# China's Fiscal Policy

As an important macroeconomic variant, the fiscal revenue and expenditure can influence the operation of the whole economic and social activities by changing the existing GDP distribution pattern, affecting the consumption and investment of enterprises and people, etc. Thus, fiscal policy has always been a primary instrument of macroeconomic regulation.

This book imports fiscal policy into the framework of macroeconomic analysis and through the analysis of the former, it unfolds the major changes of China's macroeconomic operation in the past 20 years. This book begins with China's rejoining the General Agreement on Tariffs and Trade (GATT) in the 1990s, which enabled China to deepen the reform and join the international market finally. It elaborates on the challenges China's taxation was confronted with after rejoining the GATT, including the decrease of tax revenue and higher requirements for tax reform. Then this book combs China's fiscal policies under various economic situations chronologically – tax policy against the background of deflation, proactive fiscal policy at the beginning of 21st century, macroeconomic policy options facing a complicated and volatile economy, etc. How to deal with the "new normal" of development China's economy has entered is also addressed. This book will appeal to scholars and students of economics and China's economic studies.

**Gao Peiyong** is the director of Institute of Economics, Chinese Academy of Social Sciences. His main research interests include theoretic research, policy analysis and institution design in the field of public finance and taxation.

# China Perspectives

The *China Perspectives* series focuses on translating and publishing works by leading Chinese scholars, writing about both global topics and China-related themes. It covers Humanities and Social Sciences, Education, Media and Psychology, as well as many interdisciplinary themes.

This is the first time any of these books have been published in English for international readers. The series aims to put forward a Chinese perspective, give insights into cutting-edge academic thinking in China and inspire researchers globally.

For more information, please visit www.routledge.com/series/CPH

## Existing titles

**Internet Finance in China**
Introduction and Practical Approaches
*Ping Xie, Chuanwei Zou, Haier Liu*

**Regulating China's Shadow Banks**
*Qingmin Yan, Jianhua Li*

**Internationalization of the RMB**
Establishment and Development of RMB Offshore Markets
*International Monetary Institute of the RUC*

**The Road Leading to the Market**
*Weiying Zhang*

**Peer-to-Peer Lending with Chinese Characteristics**
Development, Regulation and Outlook
*P2P Research Group Shanghai Finance Institute*

## Forthcoming titles

**Experience and Theoretical Enlightenment of China's Economic Reform**
*Zhang Yu*

**Tax Reform and Policy in China**
*Gao Peiyong*

# China's Fiscal Policy

Discretionary Approaches
and Operation Design

**Gao Peiyong**

LONDON AND NEW YORK

CHINA SOCIAL SCIENCES PRESS

This book is published with financial support from Innovation Project of CASS
Translators: Shen Jing and Lei Xia

First published 2018 by Routledge

2 Park Square, Milton Park, Abingdon, Oxfordshire OX14 4RN
52 Vanderbilt Avenue, New York, NY 10017

*Routledge is an imprint of the Taylor & Francis Group, an informa business*

First issued in paperback 2020

*British Library Cataloguing-in-Publication Data*
A catalogue record for this book is available from the British Library

*Library of Congress Cataloging-in-Publication Data*
A catalog record for this title has been requested

ISBN: 978-1-138-89957-5 (hbk)
ISBN: 978-0-367-52891-1 (pbk)

Typeset in Times New Roman
by Apex CoVantage, LLC

# Contents

# Figures

# Foreword for the Chinese edition

The Presidium of CASS (Chinese Academy of Social Sciences) Academic Division organizes the publication of Collections of the Committee Members of CASS Academic Division in order to uncover their findings of special researches on specific subjects and professions, as well as exhibit their dynamic research tracks and academic understandings after a long-term focus on a specific profession or subject. For myself, this publication is not just about the committee members of CASS academic division, but is a good opportunity to review what I have done over my scholarly research, organize my thoughts and improve my research level and quality.

After sorting out and editing my representative papers published in recent years, I locked on two clues and composed two corresponding symposiums, *Fiscal and Tax Reforms after 1994* and *Fiscal Policies in the Macroeconomic Analysis*.

The *Fiscal Policies in the Macroeconomic Analysis* present here centers on the clue of fiscal policies decided in macroeconomic situation. It consists of my representative papers on macroeconomic climate and fiscal policies published since the 1990s.

To pick up such a research angle, I have my own reasons. Starting from my undergraduate, graduate and doctoral studies, then my teaching in Tianjin University of Finance and Economics and Renmin University of China, and then my research work in CASS, I have never left the specialty of finance. Of some sort, I'm an academic with professional training in finance and long anchored in finance. After years of academic edification, I've shaped the following perceptions.

The comprehensiveness is a unique quality for which finance distinguishes itself from any other economic categories. As the fiscal revenue and expenditure provides the base for all government activities, and also links governments, enterprises and people most directly, it can cover all government functions, departments and activities and extend to all enterprises and people, all consumption and investment segments and all economic and social sectors. It means that the research on finance cannot be only about finance, but be done out of its professional limit and from a wider view.

Finance is an academic discipline of pragmatism, even for more practical purposes than any other economic discipline. All arrangements related to fiscal revenue and expenditure always get down to business by directly changing the existing interest groups, improving people's well-being, affecting economic and social development and ensuring an everlasting political stability of the state. To this end, finance has never stood alone, but is closely associated with the fervent reality throughout its development. It has never been content with theoretical ideas but emphasized the practical application of ideas by acting on them to solve realistic problems throughout its discipline building. It means research on finance cannot be only about academic theories, but perceive practices out of theoretical limit.

Basically the fiscal revenue and expenditure activities are always taken as an aggregate included into the list of the general equilibrium elements, even in the planned economy age. In the market economy time, when people are more aware of the universally true proposition that the total supply and demand are in balance, not only the fiscal revenue and expenditure becomes a more important weight in the macroeconomic equilibrium, but the macroeconomic analysis is more liable to host the discipline of finance. We should base ourselves on the macroeconomy, discuss financial issues from the macro perspective and study the financial resource allocation by macroeconomic analysis in order to obtain a sustainable and healthy development of the national economy. These are increasingly becoming the dominant orientation of the discipline development and building of finance. It means the research on finance cannot be done without macroeconomic awareness and thoughts, but must break the limit of general financial research and enter into the new era of macroeconomic analysis.

As a very important macroeconomic variant in the command of governments, fiscal revenue and expenditure can change the existing GDP distribution pattern, profoundly affecting the consumption and investment of enterprises and people, and the total supply and demand of the society, and even influencing the operation of whole economic and social activities; therefore, fiscal policy is always a primary measure of macroeconomic control under the framework of macroeconomic analysis. Rare buffer zones are left for the decisions and overall arrangements regarding fiscal policies, as they determine the success of macroeconomic policies. In some sense, the analysis of fiscal policies among macroeconomic policies is the priority among priorities in the scope of finance. It means the research on finance cannot but be done by specialized and professional economists who are known for truly excellent learning, pursuit of practical problem solving and thinking outside the box of general academics.

Given the aforementioned, I've focused on and devoted myself to research on the macroeconomy and fiscal policy for years. The dominant aim of my academic studies is to import the fiscal policy into the framework of macroeconomic analysis, and based on that, keep updated the macroeconomic ups and downs, systematically look into the implementation effects of macroeconomic policies, outline how the fiscal policy is operated and put forward the fiscal policy arrangement plans in appropriate time.

All papers collected in this symposium are compiled in publication order. They unfold all major changes of China's macroeconomy after the 1990s and the evolutionary progress of fiscal policy decision-making, the main measure of macroeconomic control and basically reflect my thoughts about fiscal policy among the macroeconomic decisions.

I would like to take this opportunity to express my gratitude to the leaders and editors of China Social Sciences Press, whose great support and help give rise to the publication of this book and I would like, also to ask for advices from peers and readers.

Gao Peiyong
July 10, 2013

# Acknowledgments

This book is a collection of evidence-based studies funded by the Innovation Program of the Chinese Academy of Social Sciences (CASS). It contains my experience regarding both the practices and the theoretical studies of China's economic development.

Here I would like to express my sincere gratitude to Ms. Shen Jing and Lei Xia, translators of this book, and Ms. Li Yanqing, for her painstaking efforts devoted to polishing the book; I also thank all of the colleagues at China Social Sciences Press for their professional and energetic support.

My particular thank goes to the CASS Innovation Translation Fund for having the book translated and published.

December, 2016

# 1 China's taxation after rejoining the GATT

China has applied to rejoin the General Agreement on Tariffs and Trade (GATT) for eight years. According to the agreement made in the Uruguay Round negotiations, the date to rejoin the GATT is coming. Rejoining the GATT means that, by deepening reform and opening wider to the outside world, the Chinese economy will become in line with international standards gradually and China will finally join the international market. With such background, like in other national economic fields, taxation will face an unprecedented challenge.

## At the initial stage of rejoining the GATT, tax revenue in China might be impacted greatly

The economic theorists generally agree on the significance of China's rejoining the GATT. On condition of international market integration, as a developing country, China has to participate in international competition and division to promote domestic economic prosperity. Rejoining the GATT – which is the biggest international trade organization in the world – helps to explore international markets, attract foreign investment, absorb foreign advanced science and technology, learn managerial experience, pick up information, deepen economic system reform and create conditions for economic take-off in China. Moreover, in the long term, the rapid national economic growth helps to cultivate and increase tax funds by driving robust growth of tax revenue.

Nevertheless, almost everything has advantages and disadvantages. The measure which is good in the long term may be bad in the short term. For China's tax revenue, an unignorable fact is that, at the initial stage of rejoining the GATT, some problems causing the decrease of tax revenue have to be solved.

- Reducing tariffs is the core of GATT, and is also China's important duty after rejoining the GATT. Since the GATT went into effect in 1948, it has held eight rounds of multilateral trade negotiation aiming to reduce tariffs. By the first seven rounds, the average tariff had decreased from 40 percent to 4–5 percent in western developed countries, and to 13–15 percent in developing countries. The Uruguay Round, the eighth round of negotiations which was completed just now, reached the agreement to further cut off tariff rates. The average tariff rate of industrial and agricultural products decreases 40 percent in six years, and the tariff rate of industrial products decreased so sharply that some products are even tax-free. As it is well known that the tariff rate in China is high, the import tariff of some products such as electronic, chemical and medical products is even 130–200 percent. In order to rejoin the GATT, China unilaterally cut off the tariffs involving more than 3000 products in October 1991, and on December 31, 1992 (it involved 225 products at the first time, and 3371 products at the second time), which decreased the tariff rate from 22.3 percent to about 15 percent. Even so, the average tariff rate in China is still higher than the average level of developing countries. The implementation of the Uruguay Round negotiations will further deepen this gap. Obviously, according to it, further decreasing the average tariff rate is the "fee to rejoin GATT" we have to bear. Once it is carried out, the average tariff rate will decrease below 10 percent, and it will impact the tariff in total more than 20 billion Yuan, which accounts for about 6.5 percent of the total tax revenue. If the increase of tax funds brought in by the increase of import products in short time can't counteract the impact of lowering average tariff rate, the tariff revenue will decrease.

• With the development of socialist construction, a relatively complete industrial system has been established gradually in China; thereinto, some departments of it have made top achievements in the world. However, the industrial technology is comparatively low in general. Nowadays, many industries are protected by maintaining a high tariff rate above 100 percent, and even administrative restrictions on import products. Once it rejoins the GATT, the tariff will decrease, the administrative restriction will be weakened, and the intellectual property will be protected; thus, many industries have to compete with import products. In the long term, it helps the industrial structural adjustment and technical transformation, and helps to improve the level of production and enhance the competitiveness in international markets, as well as promotes the enterprise mechanism transformation and establishment of a modern enterprise system in China. However, in the short term, it will impact the industrial system enjoying long-term tariff protection and non-tariff barrier protection significantly, especially the electromechanical, chemical and pharmaceutical industries; and so does the tax revenue. For example, the technologies of many electromechanical products are weak. The research on the technological level of about 3000 electromechanical products produced in the 1980s in Shanghai indicates that, 19 percent of the products could catch up with the foreign products produced in the 1930s–1940s; 76 percent of them could catch up with the foreign products produced in the 1950s–1960s; and only 5 percent of them could catch up with the foreign products produced in the 1970s. due to low technology level, although the electromechanical products made in China range widely, yet no "fist" product can compete with foreign products. The high-tech industries – such as computer, car, VCR, broadcast and TV equipment; numerically-controlled machine tools; precision processing equipment;

high-grade, precision and advanced control instrument; integrated circuits; and so on – can't compete with foreign products because of late starting, weak base and incomplete matching industries, as well as price disadvantage. Moreover, the electromechanical industry in China is depressed. Comparing 1990 with 1989, the gross electromechanical industrial output increased 2 percent and the sales revenue increased 4.2 percent, but the total pre-tax profits decreased 31.9 percent, and unprofitable enterprises doubled. In 1991, the situation didn't change much, although the scale of losses decreased, yet the total loss increased greatly.

For many chemical enterprises in China, their manufacturing technique and equipment are backward (most equipment follows the international level in the 1960s and 1970s); even though there are various protections, the costs are so high that domestic sale prices are higher than similar products in international markets. More than 10 sets of ethylene equipment and down-stream products which are being built or planned to be built, struggle to compete with similar products in international markets because of high cost caused by small-scale production (many of them just 110 kt). Moreover, the construction cycle of petrochemical enterprises is long, and international markets may change during the period of construction.

By late-mover advantage and industrial transfer, China copies many foreign advanced products, especially the main products of the chemical, pharmaceuticals and pesticide industries, which drives the whole industry to enter a new stage in the short term (many valued products are invented and created, too). According to the Uruguay Round negotiation which strengthens intellectual protection, China has to pay the duty on intellectual protection for rejoining the GATT, and it also will bring difficulties to many industries.

No need for reticence. If China's industry keeps the existing level to compete in the severely competitive after rejoining the GATT, it will be impacted significantly: the prices of many industrial products will have to be lowered. The enterprises which used to be big taxpayers in the long term will make meager profits or even take losses. Some enterprises with poor operation and bad products, as well as diseconomies of scale, are likely to be out. Furthermore, lowering the price of industrial products means that the turnover tax gaining from these products tends to decrease. The big taxpayers turn into meager-profit or unprofitable enterprises, as well as some enterprises are out during the market competition; it means that the government will lose tax revenue gained from them (at least temporarily).

• Opening service trade and bringing the service trade occupying one-fourth of the total trade in the world into GATT is one of the important terms agreed by the Uruguay Round negotiations. Compared to the service industry abroad, the service level in China is much lower than the developed countries (70 percent lower than theirs), and is lower than the average level of developing countries (40–50 percent lower than theirs). In order to rejoin the GATT, China has made a tentative promise to open service trade. Since this promise which only involves six service fields including shipping, banking, advertisement, tourism and offshore oil exploration, is not accepted by other countries, especially the developed countries, China may have to make a greater concession. On condition of this promise, no matter how greater the concession is, it is hard for the service trade in China to compete with foreign competitors after rejoining the GATT. It is unavoidable that some domestic service industries at a disadvantage will be out and the others may be in trouble. In this process, it is obvious that the tax revenue gained from service industry will suffer loss.

• After 1985, the export rebates take the place of the export loss subsidy system implemented in a long term in China. It is an important policy aiming to let export products compete in international markets with tax-exclusive prices and strengthen their competitiveness according to international practice. It is obvious that the export rebates are implemented at the cost of reducing the revenue gained from turnover tax or the tax expenditure. Besides, the amount of export rebates has positive correlation with the scale of export products. In recent years, with the enlargement of export products, the amount of export rebates tends to increase year by year. It is almost confirmed that the promotion of rejoining the GATT will increase export products and even cause it to jump. The sharp increase of export rebates causing by it will induce huge tax expenditure, and then impact the revenue gained from turnover tax.

## The rejoining of GATT sets higher requirements for tax reform in China

As the greatest tax reform in an all-round way after the foundation of the People's Republic of China, the new tax system implemented on January 1, 1994 greatly helps the tax system in China stride towards market economy. It can be said that it is also a necessary step to rejoin the GATT based on market economy. However, the reformed tax system in China is still far away from the requirements of the World Trade Organization (WTO) which will replace the GATT soon. Therefore, it still has to promote the tax reform basing on it, it is still has to promote the tax reform.

• The third term of GATT concerning the principle of national treatment regulates that different treatments between domestic products and import products on price and regulation cannot exist anymore, which means the government should provide import products with national treatment on the taxes and the decrees and regulations of sale, purchase, transport and distribution. It can be said that many aspects of our new tax system disobey this principle. For example, the current enterprise income system still classifies the enterprises as domestic and foreign enterprises. Although the income tax rates of domestic and foreign enterprises are the same, there are many differences in the system and regulation including tax deductions, standards of disbursed cost and expenditure, tax credit and so on.

The tasks of eliminating different treatments between domestic and foreign enterprises caused by tax law and establishing uniform enterprise income system have to be carried out as soon as possible during the process of rejoining the GATT.

Providing various tax preferences for special economic zones, economic development zones and coastal open cities is a special tax policy to attract foreign investment and open wider to the outside world. Although the reformed tax system reorganizes various tax reliefs carried out by local governments and prevents the tendency of tax reliefs to some extent, the framework of the policy about tax reliefs is not adjusted significantly. The essence of special tax policy aiming at different regions and different enterprises is a kind of different treatment. According to the principle of GATT, it must be canceled. In practice, local governments' tax preference for foreign enterprise and development zone should first be abolished. Based on it, the difference of tax preference on areas should be narrowed gradually, and finally, tax preference on areas should be changed to tax preference on industries or businesses.

- The GATT is based on the market economy. Market price and free competition are the footstone of GATT. It means that the development of price reform in China directly relates with the success of rejoining the GATT. And for the price reform, it is very important to change the turnover tax from "taxes included in price" to "taxes not included in price".

In order to match the traditional planned price, the system of "taxes included in price" is carried out through turnover tax in the long term in China. For the reformed turnover tax system, besides that the tax not included in price is carried out through added-value tax, the other two items of taxation – consumption tax and business tax – are still levied by taxes included in price. On condition of the system of taxes included in price, turnover tax is a part of planned price, and if the tax is levied by tax-inclusive price, the change of tax rate will not change the price but the corporate profit. Its purpose is to match the price policy to regulate the profitability of different products; "high tax matching high price, and low tax matching low price" is the brief summary of the system of taxes included in price. However, as rejoining the GATT requires opening the price of almost all products including domestic and import products, the incompatibility between the system of taxes included in price and market price system will be obvious day by day. For the system of taxes included in price, the tax is included in price. Even though the supply and demand change, tax is fixed. The price can't reflect real market supply and demand and its tendency, thus the price can hardly play the role of "market barometer". In particular, when tax rate is regulated, the change of price only reflects the change of tax revenue. The problem that market signal comes apart market supply and demand will become more severe.

It looks that, for the turnover tax in China, it is necessary to totally change the system of taxes included in price matching planned price to the system of taxes not included in price matching market price. It is different from the system of taxes included in price in which tax is a part of price. In the system of taxes not included in price, turnover tax which is not a part of tax is levied by tax exclusive price, and the tax is the added value of price. Taxes unhook the formation mechanism of price, and they are decided in different places. Market supply and demand decide price, and tax is the product of government's economic policy. The boundary line between tax and price is clear and each one performs its own functions, and the price actually reflects the change of market supply and demand. Basically, it is the basic condition that market mechanism plays the role of resource distribution.

It is necessary to point out that, proposing to change the taxes included in price to taxes not included in price and let the tax unhook the formation mechanism of price doesn't mean giving up tax regulation on production and consumption. On the contrary, tax regulation is necessary. However, in the writer's opinion, tax regulation must be the "second regulation" based on market regulation, and tax regulation can't disturb or distort the formation mechanism of market price.

- Policy transparency is an important principle for GATT. According to it, as the contracting party, the laws, regulations, policy measurements, rules and corresponding data and material about foreign trade should be opened to the other parties. To establish the "transparency" of the tax system, it should be noticed that it has made great progress on the new tax system and made significant achievement in the construction of a legal system concerning taxes. The problem is how to follow this tendency to normalize the construction of a legal system concerning taxes and unify the tax policy throughout the whole country.

For example, it is well known that the force of law concerning tax is poor in China. Although there are various reasons, including few formal decrees about tax and incomplete legal system concerning tax, the most important reasons are lax enforcement and flexible interpretation about tax law. It is obvious that, if these problems can't be solved effectively, even it speeds up the legislative process of tax law and completes the legal system concerning tax, the "transparency" of the tax system is just a meaningless term. Therefore, on condition that various tax codes are issued successively and tend to be advanced, solving the problems about lax enforcement and flexible interpretation about tax law is the task which should be put on the agenda as soon as possible.

The existence of large "indigenous methods" concerning tax revenue reflects that tax system in China lacks transparency. Some time ago, in order to attract foreign investment, many local governments issued relevant rules and regulations to provide tax preferences; thus, there was a new climate to reduce tax on enterprises and allow them to retain more profits in the whole country. It is a significant example. Obviously, with no uniformity or seriousness of tax system and no transparency of tax system, it is hard to build a good image of unified government decree and stable policy, and it even hinders the process of rejoining the GATT. Therefore, in order to rejoin the GATT, it is necessary to unify tax policy and centralize legislative authority of tax to form a complete, explicit, authoritative, detailed and practical tax code as soon as possible for tax reform.

- On condition of severe market after rejoining the GATT, many enterprises in manufacturing, service and other industries will be unprecedentedly impacted. It is unavoidable that some enterprises might have to close down, to be merged, or even to go bankrupt. The consequence is that unemployment will increase greatly, and the lives of those who suffer survival crisis after bankruptcy should be taken into consideration. In order to solve this problem, the urgent affair is to build a social security system relying on social security tax as the main capital source.

In fact, with the development of reform of the enterprise system, establishing a social security system has been proposed repeatedly. And rejoining the GATT causes this issue to come to a head. It means that establishing a social security system is not only the requirement for rejoining the GATT, but is basically also the important measure to develop a socialist market economy. Because the establishment of a social security system needs a corresponding capital source, it is necessary to follow the standard international practice and begin to collect earmarked taxes called social security tax when facing the financial constraints, as well as tax loss caused by rejoining the GATT.

(Originally published in Taxation Research, Vol.12, 1994)

# 2 The evolving foreign-related preferential tax policy in China

## 1

In general, China's foreign-related preferential tax policy, which is the outcome of reform and opening-up policy, was initiated at the end of the 1970s and the beginning of the 1980s. The background is that market-oriented reform was promoted in the whole country. It had achieved the agreement that opening to the outside world was the basic state policy. In order to attract great foreign capital as well as speed up the utilization of it, China went the way of "promoting opening with preference" under that international environment. For the tax system, it provided foreign investment with a series of tax preferences to reduce FIE (foreign invested enterprise) tax burden, which was significantly lower than that of domestic enterprises. Moreover, for the construction of special economic zones, economic and technological development zones, open coastal economic areas, high-tech development zones, tariff-free zones, and so on, it designed and formed a multi-level pattern of foreign-related tax preference, which could be described as "special economic zone – economic and technological development zone – open coastal economic area – other specific zones – general inland zone".

The complete implementation of foreign-related preferential tax policy and the confirmation of multi-level pattern about foreign-related tax preference had promoted economic and social development greatly:

- The FIE developed from nothing and flourished. During 1979–1995, number of the contracted foreign direct investment (FDI) projects was 258,788 (average 15,223 projects per year), and the aggregate of those projects totaled $395.86 billion. Thereafter, the number of contracted FDI projects was 47,549 in 1994 and 37,011 in 1995, and the aggregate of those projects totaled $82.68 billion and $91.28 billion, respectively. The FIE has become an important power to ensure China's high-speed economic development, and played an important role in economic and social life.
- With the inburst of FIE, China's textile industry developed well first, followed by the household appliance industry and other light industries; in addition, the production of computer parts developed from nothing and became the new growth point of high-tech industry, and the automobile

industry also started. It incentivized some industries to upgrade rapidly and even directly drove to establish several brand new industries.

- As the enterprise fully adhered to the principle of market economy, the development of FIE established a reference of modern enterprises for developing a market economy. This demonstration effect drove the reform to rebuild the micro base of domestic enterprises.
- Most importantly, the formation and extension of the pattern of opening to the outside world promoted the planned economy to shift to a market economy to great extent, as well as the development of market economic systems. The core to establish the framework of a market economy was to confirm that market allocation was the mainstay of resource allocation. Opening to the outside world meant that China's economic entities had to trade and operate all over the world. The international practice about resource allocation mechanisms was transmitted to China successfully, which induced a series of market-oriented reforms to adapt to the outside world.

## 2

At the beginning of reform and opening up, the development of a market economy and opening to the outside world just started, and all conditions needed to be improved. The complete foreign-related preferential tax policy and multi-level pattern of foreign-related tax preference could perform well on attracting foreign capital instantly in short time. However, with the deepening of market-oriented reform and the extension of opening to the outside world, the function of complete foreign-related preferential tax policy and multi-level pattern of foreign-related tax preference becomes weak and faces more and more severe challenges:

- One of the souls of a market economy is fair competition. There must be well-regulated and fair competition among the economic entities as a condition of a market economy, rather than differential treatment which will cause unfair conditions according to ownership, administrative subordination or investment resource. The current foreign-related preferential tax policy obviously disobeys those requirements. For example, although the nominal rates of income tax of both domestic enterprise and FIE are 33 percent, the FIE founded in certain areas such as special economic zones, economic and technological development zones, and so on, can be taxed by the rate of 15 percent, 24 percent, or even 10 percent. At the same time, the preferential tax policy provided for new domestic enterprise is to reduce or exempt income tax in the first one or two years since establishment (or exempt it for the first year then reduce half of it for the second and third years); however, FIE can exempt income tax in the first two years and reduce half of it in the following three years since it starts to make profit (even exempt it in the first five years and then reduce half of it in the following five years). The result is that the tax burden of income tax of FIE is less than one-third of domestic enterprise. The tax burden with significant difference hinders

fair competition between FIE and domestic enterprise, and reasonable allocation of resources, and hinders domestic enterprises from conducting foreign
trade under almost the same conditions; in addition, it even causes some
circumforaneous FIEs, which damage national interest severely.

- Based on providing general tax preference for FIEs, different tax preferences
are provided in different regions according to "special economic zone –
economic and technological development zone – open coastal economic
area – other specific zones – general inland zone" classifications. Since there
are various levels in this system and the geographic boundaries are hard to
identify, the location of productive force among regions is influenced, as is
the managerial work in practice. Especially for central and western China,
there are bad objective conditions, weak infrastructure and out-of-date information, which are disadvantages for economic development. Compared with
central and western regions, eastern regions have convenient traffic and
unimpeded flow of information, so there are advantages for economic development. Foreign-related preferential tax policy inclined to eastern coastal
regions, for example, will cause negative effect on narrowing the gap of
economic development among regions. This negative effect is bad for balanced development among regions; moreover, with political consideration,
if things keep going on like this, it may intensify the gap between rich and
poor regions, which impacts national security negatively in the long term.
- Too much tax preference causes the loss of national fiscal revenue from two
aspects. On the one hand, a significant amount of tax evasion and avoidance
directly causes a reduction in fiscal revenue. On the other hand, complex
and various tax preferences provide space to evade and avoid tax for taxpayers (especially FIE), which causes a great loss of national tax revenue.

Additionally, on condition that government expenditure increases greatly and there
is great "gap" between fiscal revenue and expenditure, the loss of national fiscal
revenue caused by great tax preferences causes the governments at all levels to
explore other fiscal sources in the form of charge to cover the "gap". Moreover,
for self-controlled revenue and expenditure, there is a tide in the whole country to
make chargeable items by governments at all levels themselves. Because they are
nonstandard charges with low transparency, and this phenomenon tends to spread
and the scale tends to expand, it further impacts tax base, intensifies the loss of
national tax revenue, and makes the government revenue mechanism and even the
whole national income distribution mechanism nonstandard.

- Tax burden is one of the reasons influencing foreign investments, but not
the only one. Additionally, the infrastructure, government efficiency and
service level, maturity of law and regulation, and so on, are important factors influencing whether foreign investment can make a profit and how much
profit it can make. Therefore, even though paying attention to tax preference
to merely attract foreign investment can be effective in the short term, it
will hinder the attraction of foreign capital in great scale in the long term

for the limited effect of tax preference. No matter what aspects considered from, the effect of tax preference is exaggerated to some extent for these years, and the construction of the other aspects is ignored to some extent. It also can be said that the comparative lag of the constriction of infrastructure, legal system, government efficiency and service level, and so on, restricts the opening to the outside world.

## 3

So far, it is proper to draw a conclusion like this: China's foreign-related preferential tax policy with the features of complete tax preference for all FIEs and multi-level foreign-related tax preference for different FIEs has become one of the reasons hindering the deepening of market-oriented reform and the expansion of opening to the outside world. Therefore, it must rebuild and standardize the current multi-level pattern of foreign-related tax preference.

But how to do it?

- Tax reform indicates the tendency of "neutralization" all over the world in the middle of the 1980s, which changes the understanding of foreign-related preferential tax policy greatly and decreases the expectation about the effect of tax preference. The orientation of China's foreign-related preferential tax policy is that it should "properly" utilize tax preference to control the tax preference provided to FIEs at a "proper" level. It includes two aspects of meaning: first, for the aspect of development direction, China's foreign-related preferential tax policy should approach the principle of national treatment. At this point, so many tax preferences don't match the principle of national treatment that they must be standardized and reduced. Second, approaching the principle of national treatment doesn't mean abolishing foreign-related preferential tax policy completely, because the basic idea of national treatment principle is to provide foreign product (enterprise) with treatment not worse than domestic product (enterprise). At this point, it is not only necessary – but also feasible – to design and retain some foreign-related preferential tax policies.
- Taking the management of foreign-related preferential tax policy as precondition, it shifts the emphasis of preference to national industrial policy to unify all the aspects of preference including direction, aim, range, content, form and method. The future selection of foreign-related preferential tax policy should gradually shift to provide complete tax preference for all FIEs and multi-level foreign-related tax preference for different FIEs according to the basic requirements of national industrial policy. For the development of different industries, efficiency first should be embodied, and necessary preferential tax policy should be implemented to guide foreign investment to those industries which need to be encouraged and developed urgently.
- It should evaluate the effect of foreign-related preferential tax policy clearly and consider the construction of integrated environment for foreign

investment. As was is said previously, integrated environment includes many aspects which depend on each other; the lack of any aspect will damage the environment for foreign investment. The urgent thing is to rebuild and standardize foreign-related preferential tax policy and to improve the other aspects. Especially, it should try hard to shift government's concept, increase government efficiency, improve legal construction, and cultivate marketing systems. To some extent, at present, the attraction of improving any aspect of foreign investment environment is greater than single tax preference.

- Attracting foreign investment and developing the national economy should be connected effectively. Based on the same tax law applicable to domestic and foreign enterprises, it should shift from providing complete preference to certain preference for FIEs. On condition of unfair competition between domestic and foreign enterprises, especially state-owned enterprises' severe difficulty, it should take action to unify the income tax of domestic and foreign enterprises to create a market environment with equal competition as soon as possible. As the same time, it should provide certain projects of FIEs proper tax preference to strengthen taxes' guiding function on investment direction.

- It should carry out total quantity control about foreign-related preferential tax policy strictly and bring tax preference into the overall framework of the balance of national fiscal revenue and expenditure. The tax preference, no matter aimed at domestic enterprise or FIE, fundamentally means the loss or decrease of fiscal revenue. The loss or decrease of fiscal revenue will influence the balance of fiscal expenditure. Therefore, if it takes foreign-related preferential tax policy as special regulation, the total amount must be controlled. It should confirm the condition of preference in the limit of fixed amount. The limit of total amount can't be broken through to avoid influencing the balance of national fiscal revenue and expenditure and the macro regulation.

Further, the total quantity control about foreign-related preferential tax policy is also an important measure to stop widespread flooding of government fees, and to standardize government revenue mechanisms and national income distribution mechanisms.

(Originally published in *International Taxation in China*, Vol.8, 1997)

# 3 Overall accounting and detailed accounting

## Consideration of China's current fiscal policy

### Overall accounting: based on the steady development of economy and society

An overall accounting should be conducted, rather than partly. Sometimes, steady development of economy and society should be pursued at the cost of unbalanced fiscal revenue and expenditure if necessary. It is not only an important principle for modern economics, but also a basic principle for China's fiscal policy since it started reform and opening-up policy.

China's economic structural reform which starts from the domain of distribution confirms the reform thought of "decentralization of power and transfer of profits" at the very start. On the one hand, decentralization of power and transfer of profits require carrying out tax cuts and transfer of profits for microeconomic entities, and then stimulation of all the entities' initiative by reducing their fiscal share of national income distribution; on the other hand, on condition of increasing fiscal expenditure, it has to pave the way for various reforms. The result is that frequent fiscal deficits and growing national debt accompany economic structural reform. As it is, China has gone the way of achieving successful economic structural reform at the cost of unbalanced fiscal revenue and expenditure for 20 years.

The current social and economic situation causes difficulty in fiscal policy: the lack of total social demand threatens the target of economic growth this year. On condition that the threat of Asian financial crisis spreads that it even slows international trade and economic growth, the most effective way to promote economic growth is to boost domestic consumption, apparently. Although boosting domestic consumption can be achieved by household consumption and enterprise investment, it is difficult to change lackluster sales, decreasing price and low consumption demand greatly in the near future, on condition of slow growth of household income and increasing anticipated consumption expenditure; recently, although stated-owned economic entities' fixed investments increase, the foreign investments, collective investments and individual investments decrease – yet the overall investment demand is insufficient to get rid of sluggish growth. Therefore, what government can do is to implement expansionary fiscal policy which lets government play the part of investing entity to invest directly. Certainly, the increase of government investment takes corresponding expansion of fiscal expenditure as precondition. For severe fiscal revenue and expenditure in China, the expansion of fiscal expenditure means more serious fiscal difficulties. However, national economic development can't leave the expansion of domestic demand; and the scale of current domestic demand is decided by the amount of fiscal input. Therefore, in order to stimulate domestic demand and ensure the realization of full-year economic growth target, issuing treasury bonds totaling 100 billion Yuan to increase infrastructure construction becomes the natural choice of fiscal policy.

As the measures are taken to get successful economic structural reform, by overall accounting, issuing treasury bonds to increase infrastructure construction is the worthy price for fiscal revenue and expenditure. It can be seen that if no fiscal policy deals with the lack of total demand on condition of severe fiscal revenue and expenditure for fiscal revenue and expenditure itself, economic downturn would decrease fiscal revenue and reduce fiscal expenditure, resulting in sluggish economic growth and even economic contraction. The result is that not only could the fiscal revenue and expenditure not be improved, but also further economic depression occurs in a vicious circle of fiscal revenue and expenditure. On the contrary, if temporarily increasing fiscal difficulty is taken as the necessary cost to stimulate economy, it will bring in steady national economic development, and the fiscal revenue and expenditure will improve gradually based on economic development.

## Detailed accounting: envisioning the current severe fiscal revenue and expenditure

Overall accounting helps to balance priorities and realize integral profits without the limit of departments, but it doesn't mean that we can know nothing about the cost of realizing macroeconomic targets. It means that we should calculate the cost of expansionary fiscal policy.

Issuing treasury bonds will certainly increase the existing scale of treasury bonds. The research on the cost of expansionary fiscal policy can use the shift of the scale of treasury bonds as a guide. Although there are several indexes to measure the scale of treasury bonds, two of them are generally used. The first is the proportion of aggregate treasury bonds in GDP (gross domestic product) of the same year. It pays attention to the stock of treasury bonds to reflect the proportional relation between the aggregate treasury bonds and the GDP in the same year, and it is also called "debt-to-GDP ratio". The other is the proportion of the issued amount of treasury bonds in the fiscal expenditure of the same year. It pays attention to the flow of treasury bonds to reflect the fiscal expenditure's dependence on fiscal revenue, and it is called "the degree of fiscal expenditure's dependence on debt".

For the first index, until the end of 1997, the aggregate of unpaid treasury bonds totaled 592.88 billion Yuan, which accounted for 7.93 percent of the GDP in the same year. According to this year's confirmed amount of issuing treasury bonds (6508.6 = 2808.6 + 2700 + 1000) deducting the capital of matured treasury bonds (176.145 billion Yuan – it is calculated that 75 percent of the total treasury bonds, including both capital and interest, totaled 234.86 billion Yuan), it can be estimated that, until the end of 1998, the aggregate treasury bond will reach 1076.6 billion

Yuan, which accounts for 13.3 percent of the GDP in the same year (the economic growth rate is estimated to be 8 percent). Comparing with 1997, debt-to-GDP ratio increases 5.37 percent.

For the latter index, in 1997, issued treasury bonds totaled 247.683 billion Yuan, which occupied 22.29 percent of the national fiscal expenditure (central and local governments' fiscal expenditure in total) and 55.76 percent of the central fiscal expenditure (only central government's fiscal expenditure). Based on the confirmed issuing treasury bond (valued 650.86 billion Yuan), it adjusts the national budget outlays (10143.68 + 2348.6 + 2700 + 1000) and central budget outlays (2752.52 + 2348.6 + 2700 + 1000); it estimates that, in 1998, the degree of dependency of national finance and central finance on debt would be 40.19 percent and 73.95 percent, respectively. Comparing with 1997, these two indexes increase 17.9 percent and 18.19 percent, respectively.

These two indexes indicate that, in order to carry out expansionary fiscal policy, China has to face higher debt-to-GDP ratio and higher degree of dependence on debt.

The more severe fact is that the increase of issuing treasury bonds not only brings in the increase of the degree of dependence on debt in that year, but also brings in greater issuance of treasury bonds for several years even forming vicious circle of "issuing more and more treasury bonds" under the current situation that the repayment of capital and interest of treasury bonds totally depends on borrowing new money. In fact, the vicious circle has occurred in China. From 1993–1998, the yearly growth rate of issuance of treasury bond was 58.99 percent, 31.87 percent, 26.95 percent, 28.71 percent, and 162.78 percent, respectively. Except the rate of this year, the yearly average growth rate is 36.62 percent; in addition, the situation in this year is special that it is something else.

It can be seen that, for several years or even more, difficulties in fiscal revenue and expenditure will be more severe. Only if we pay much attention to this issue and take precautions to arrange all aspects accordingly can we get through it. While the macroeconomic benefit is considered at the cost of fiscal revenue and expenditure difficulty, it will become a virtuous circle as soon as possible. And it is proper to consider detailed accounting of the cost of fiscal policy.

## Staying firmly rooted in the present while looking ahead to the future

On the one hand, expansionary fiscal policy is necessary for sustainable and stable development of national economy; on the other hand, expansionary fiscal policy will cause more severe fiscal difficulty. Considering that, the only choice may be staying firmly rooted in the present while looking ahead to the future.

First, the fixed sum is for a fixed purpose that the revenue gained by issuing treasury bonds must be used to support infrastructure construction. The utilization of the funds collected by treasury bonds must differ from general fiscal funds. Since it is issued for the purpose of infrastructure construction, it must be used only to support infrastructure construction, not for other projects.

Second, advancing the management of the funds collected by treasury bonds and paying attention to the usage efficiency is necessary. Stimulating the economy by expansionary fiscal policy doesn't mean lavish utilization of funds. On the contrary, no matter what it is, every item of expenditure should be arranged reasonably to get maximum benefits at minimum cost.

Third, completing the tax system to avoid tax evasion and increase tax revenue is necessary. Basically, with the constraint of exiting fiscal revenue and expenditure, there is substitutional relation between the form of recurrent fiscal revenue – tax revenue and the form of compensable fiscal revenue; treasury bonds that one increases will bring in the decrease of the other. In order to try best to reduce the issuance of treasury bonds, it is necessary and possible to collect tax –as it should be. Therefore, fiscal policy should start from the completion of a tax system to avoid tax evasion to minimize the loss of tax.

Fourth, observing the economic situation carefully to adjust policies accordingly in time is necessary to carry out expansionary fiscal policy against the background of lacking total social demand and slow economic growth. With the change of economic situation, the orientation of fiscal policy must be shifted accordingly. Therefore, while expansionary fiscal policy is carried out, the economic situation must be observed carefully. Once economic recovery appears, the stimulation of fiscal policy should be weakened accordingly, or it should even go back to the way of moderately tight fiscal policy.

(Originally published in *People's Tribune*,
Vol.10, 1998)

# 4 Selection of tax policy against the background of deflation

## Discussion of current tax cut claims

In 1998, there were disputes about whether deflation appeared, and there were many suggestions to stimulate the economy by various measures including tax cuts. In 1999, during conditions of falling prices, lack of consumption and slow economic growth, more and more people made the judgment that China's economy was in or tended to be in a stage of deflation. Therefore, after the central government decided to further carry out expansionary fiscal policy and took a series of supporting measures, the appeal about tax cuts appeared again. It seems that in China, the unavoidable problem is what kind of tax policy can be chosen to deal with severe deflation.

### Tax cuts: strict definition must be given

Strictly, tax cuts mean to reduce tax revenue to decrease the tax burden of the enterprises or residents by adjusting existing tax policy. The meaning includes three levels. First, it should be realized by adjusting or changing tax reform formally, such as by reducing tax categories, lowering tax rates, or narrowing the tax base, rather than non-standard administrative behaviors decided by any leader or any Party and government department. Second, it aims to create a long-term systematic arrangement but not a short-term expedient. Third, in the short term, the direct result is that the total tax revenue decreases or tax burden of the enterprises and residents decreases – or at least, the proportion of tax revenue in GDP decreases.

Comparing with the suggestions about tax cuts, especially the micro operation, it may be seen that many discussions can't exert the functions of tax cuts mentioned previously, or can't match them well.

First, so far, many suggestions about tax cuts are informal administrative operations rather than formal systematic arrangements. For example, suggestions include: to provide the enterprises in tough times with special preference of temporary duty free status; to allow the enterprise investments to offset against income taxes; to provide the same preference as foreign investments to the investment fields encouraged by governments' industrial policies; and even to allow the enterprises to delay to pay tax, and so on. How to carry out these preferences depends on the tax system's flexibility in operation (National Development and Plan Commission, 1999). It means that it can be considerately used by government to adjust measures suitable for local conditions. It reminds us the tide of tax cuts all over the country before 1994. The lesson of it is still fresh. It should be noted that taking tax cuts as the tool to adjust economic and social development fits the regulation of market economic development. However, the operation of it must be limited in the frame of the existing tax system, or be realized by adjusting or changing the existing tax system, rather than going beyond this frame or paying no attention to formal procedure. Otherwise, against the background of existing national condition, it may trigger new tide of optional tax cuts. Therefore, even though tax cuts are unavoidable, the operation of them must be standardized. It is inadvisable to follow the tracks of an overthrown chariot for temporary demand, or else it will block the reform and development in the long term.

The following conclusions may be made according to the previous analysis. First, in the frame of the existing tax system, increasing tax revenue by advancing the management of taxation, reducing tax evasion, payment of taxes owed and fighting against corruption doesn't mean tax increases. Second, for the same reason, if it doesn't adjust or change the existing tax system, the reduction of tax revenue caused by the spread of tax evasion doesn't mean tax cuts.

Second, although there are differences among suggestions about tax cuts, their starting points are the same. By tax cuts, it is sought to increase enterprises' and residents' disposable income to stimulate investment and consumption to drive economic growth. The problem is that the change of tax system is a serious issue, but not an expedient. Whether tax cuts are an effective tool to regulate the economy depends on judgments about economic trends in the future. If deflation is considered to be a long-term economic phenomenon, tax cuts are acceptable. However, if deflation is a short-term economic phenomenon but inflation will be a serious threat in long term, tax cuts are not good choice. Further, economic cycle fluctuation is a regulative phenomenon which can't be avoided. The design of a tax system tied with economic cycle fluctuation will cause the tax system to lose its own feature of stability. It is just like the selection of measures to cover fiscal deficit: borrowing money can cover fiscal deficit, so does increasing taxes; since the deficit is a kind of short-term economic phenomenon but not normal economic life, and it is hard to control the scale and frequency, the adjustable measure of debt is the better way to solve this problem than the comparatively stable method of tax increase. It is feared that the benefits and costs of tax cuts adopted to reduce the influence of economic cycle fluctuation are hard to estimate. Therefore, even it has to carry out tax cuts, the implementation must be a long-term strategy to support institutional innovation. The short-term measures, especially emergency measures, mustn't damage the long-term aim of institutional structure regulation.

By the way, the Reagan administration's tax cuts and the tide of tax cuts driven by it in the 1980s were definitely not short-term emergency measures but long-term consideration about creating an institutional environment beneficial for private investment. On the contrary, in order to deal with inflation, this tax system levying heavy tax on investment during the tax reform in 1994 is a short-term measure. Today, inflation is replaced by deflation, and it has become an untimely policy that has to be changed.

Third, most suggestions about tax cuts think that they will not decrease tax revenue, but increase tax revenue. However, leaving aside the long-term effect of tax cuts, the implementation of tax cuts must accompany a decrease of current tax revenue. Looking at the situation of taxation in China, it may be seen that, although the absolute amount of tax revenue tends to increase in recent years, the relative amount of tax revenue – the proportion of tax revenue in GDP – is always low. In 1998, although it made tremendous efforts, the proportion of aggregated tax revenue (926.28 billion Yuan) in GDP in the same year (7.9553 trillion Yuan) was only more than 11.6 percent. The tax burden level like that is very low comparing with most developing countries, let alone developed countries (Gao Peiyong, 1999a). Moreover, the Chinese government's functions are the most diversified in the world. As condition of it, if tax cuts are carried out, the first thing necessary is to find out proper countermeasures to face the current tax revenue effect brought by them. Therefore, even though we have to carry out tax cuts, they must be implemented on condition of leaving enough space to regulate tax revenue or cut government expenditure at the same time. The government should not look forward to the increase of tax revenue in future but ignore the current fact.

## Choice about idea and reality

If only tax cuts are concerned, nobody will object to it. We always want the enterprises and residents to bear minimum tax burden at any time. However, once tax cuts have correlation with fiscal expenditure or government function, the discussion about it must be prudent.

Since the implementation of reform and opening-up policy, the topic about how to go through fiscal difficulties is always hot. Looking forward, fiscal difficulty will not ease, but will tend to be severe. In the current situation, attention must be paid to these changes related to fiscal expenditures:

First, fiscal expenditure for supporting state-owned enterprise (SOE) reform. The difficulties about SOE reform and development have become the focus of the Party and masses. If this problem can't be solved effectively, the whole economic structural reform and economic and social development will be damaged. However, it should be noted that the solution takes fiscal support as condition. According to the Central Committee of the Communist Party of China's Decisions about SOE Reform and Development (1999), SOE's technological advance and industrial upgrade needs soft loans, payroll cuts to improve efficiency, re-employment, and fiscal support of social security; the social function separated from SOE must be undertaken by fiscal revenue; and the debt-to-equity swap aiming to solve SOE's difficulty caused by heavy debt needs fiscal support. Predictably, with the implementation of these measures, fiscal expenditure may jump.

Second, repayment of loans. Different from international practice, China's repayment of loans totally depends on new debt. It means that not only the capital of national debt must be repaid by new debt, but also the interest on it would be listed in recurrent fiscal expenditure which must be repaid by new debt. For the budget, the repayment of loans and the corresponding revenue gained by debt are also excluded from the recurrent budget; thus there is the "third budget" – debt budget, which is different from recurrent budget and constructive budget. The direct result is that annual fiscal expenditure becomes greater and greater, which also causes a vicious circle as the scale of treasury bonds becomes greater and greater. Apparently, it seems that the repayment of loans can break away from the annual fiscal budget, and the corresponding revenue gained by debt can form an independent self-circulative system. However, once it goes deeper, it can be found that – without the support of corresponding fiscal revenue whose subject is taxation – the issuance of treasury bonds, just like the wood without root, can't survive. The severe fact is that with the expansion of repayment of loans and the implementation of proactive fiscal policy of enlarged fiscal expenditure supported by issuing new treasury bonds, the proportions of the scale of treasury bond in GDP and the central fiscal expenditure are large. In 1998, the proportions of these two were 8.29 percent (659.1 billion Yuan/7.9553 trillion Yuan) and 76.89 percent (659.1 billion Yuan/857.1 billion Yuan). The scale of treasury bonds, as well as the dependence of government finance and overall economic and social development on them, indicate that the significance of issuing treasury bonds is beyond itself (Gao Peiyong, 1999b). Whether it can promote the treasury bonds with planned scale successfully will become the great thing concerning national political stability and economic development.

Third, defense expenditure. Although peace and development is becoming the mainstream of the world, the Kosovo crisis and "Taiwan independence" movement indicate that the international situation is not so peaceful and the surroundings seem to be depressing. Facing that serious challenge, China has to improve its strength, and national defense construction is the most important thing. Improving national defense construction will increase fiscal expenditure. Moreover, according to China's current national defense construction and its target, the increase of fiscal expenditure will be significant in the next few years.

Fourth, science and education expenditure. Comparing with the actual requirement and the average level in the world, China's fiscal expenditure in science and education is weak. For now, China can't reach the aim made by the *China Education Reform and Development Guidelines* in 1993 that fiscal education expenditure should reach 4 percent at the end of the century. The gap between the aim and reality even tends to be widening. With the coming knowledge economics age, scientific and talent competitions become more and more severe, and the appeal to increase science and education expenditure continues, so the decision-making level and financial sector suffer more and more pressure. If things go on like this, it is imperative to increase science and education expenditure. In addition, since the formation of a new administration, the investment in science and education increases year by year. According to the tendency, as well as the influence of measurements aiming to stimulate economy such as booming enrollment in colleges and universities, science and education expenditure will increase greatly.

There are many items of expenditure like these. Of course, it is possible to reduce expenditure, such as administrative expenditure; yet, in any case, for the overall condition, the total fiscal expenditure will increase rather than decrease.

The purpose in describing China's severe fiscal situation in detail is to indicate that there are only two results caused by tax cuts on condition that fiscal expenditure can't decrease but increase: the first is that it has to increase the scale of treasury bond to fill up the revenue gap caused by tax cuts; the second is that it has to shift fiscal policy, which is difficult to sustain. Further, regardless of the result, the economic and social development will be threatened.

## The influence of tax cuts on stimulating the economy should not be overvalued

Now that the influence of macroeconomic policies is always overvalued, the influence of tax cuts on stimulating economy also tends to be overvalued. Against the background of current national conditions, the suggestions about tax cuts can be considered from the following views.

After Keynes, it was very popular to believe that government intervention could eliminate economic fluctuation. The facts indicated that this was just the expectation, but there are still many suggestions overvaluing government intervention. When the Southeast Asian financial crisis impacted China, it was eager to avoid the influence on China's economy by expanding monetary supply. Once monetary policy didn't work well and the central government decided to carry out proactive fiscal policy and stimulate domestic demand by expanding government investment on infrastructure, there was optimism that China's economy could get out of a slump. When the fiscal policy aiming to increase government expenditure couldn't boost consumer spending as expected and the deflation tended to be more severe, there were many complaints, for example, that government only paid attention to fiscal expenditure but not fiscal revenue, that there was contradiction between fiscal policies of expenditure and revenue, and even that the fiscal policy was "lame". It seems that so long as government carries out proper macroeconomic policies, it could get rid of deflation and come back to prosperity. In general, people don't prepare themselves mentally to accept economic fluctuation which is unavoidable and serious. According to recent research by Professor Huang Da (Huang Da, 1999), economic growth with no fluctuation is impossible, and the power which causes the fluctuation originating from the economy itself can't be eliminated by human intervention. Realizing this rule helps us to connect the expectation about tax cuts with economic cycle fluctuation: no matter what macroeconomic policies adopted by the government, various policies including tax cuts could only relieve economic fluctuation – but not eliminate it. This is the first point.

The implementation of macroeconomic policies for more than one year helps to understand the complexity of China's current economic situation. One of the most important things is that China's current deflation is different from general deflation. General deflation is a regulative economic phenomenon accompanied by economic cycle fluctuation within an existing system. But the current deflation in China is happening during the process of economic structural reform. Besides the basic features of general deflation, there is uncertainty about systematic expectations. Therefore, simply carrying out the countermeasures applicable to general deflation to solve China's current problems may not work well. For example, in general, after government increases expenditure (especially the expenditure to pay wages), the disposable income of residents will increase more or less. More money will result in more consumption (regardless of the proportion), and not all the increased income is deposited. However, abnormal phenomena appear in China. No matter how much expenditure government increases, the effect of stimulating consumption is just like looking at a flower in fog – it doesn't work well. The reason is that it has direct correlation with peoples' certain expectations about the future in the reform era. Though people feel income growth, they find that with proceeding of the reform, many kinds of welfare have disappeared for example, the house must be paid, so does the education, and welfare for the aged and medical benefits are uncertain. At the same time, the expectation about future tends to be not good. These factors, such as uncertain expectations about income and expenditure, and the traditional Chinese prudent attitude, decide that the enterprises and residents will tend to reduce consumption by themselves. Against this background, it is sure that the effect of macroeconomic policies will be weakened. The effect of increasing expenditure is not as positive as wanted, not to mention the indirect function of tax cuts. Although tax cuts can increase disposable income of enterprises and residents, it is uncertain how much the disposable income increased by tax cuts will be used for investment and consumption. This is the second point.

In general, the theoretical supports of tax cuts come from Keynesian demand regulation or supply-side economics, both based on western countries' tax systems. It is well known that income tax is the majority of western countries' tax systems. Although it tends to increase the proportion of turnover tax, the overall frame of the tax systems is still the same. One of the features of income tax is that it is a suitable tool to regulate an economy. No matter the automatic stabilizer, the discretionary decision-making – or the Laffer Theorem, which insists that tax cuts will not decrease but increase tax revenue – plays its part by the mechanism of income tax. However, the tax system in China is totally different from that. In 1998, the proportion of revenue gained by added-value tax, consumption tax and business tax in total tax revenue was nearly 70 percent. Compared with income tax, the tax system in which turnover tax is the majority is not a good tool to regulate the economy. The reason is simply that it is indirect tax and its mechanism is indirect, and the final impact is not easy to control, and so on. Therefore, the tax cuts which had significant effect on western countries in the 1980s will not work well in China as it is expected. This is the third point.

From the economic cycle fluctuation to the specificity of deflation in China, and then to the current tax system in China, it seems to be confirmed that, although tax cuts that may play a part in defusing deflation in China can't be denied, comparing it with the costs – the intensified fiscal difficulty and the threatened economic and social development – the loss outweighs the gain.

## Tax policy should be selected with an eye to its own features

If these facts are analyzed comprehensively, one can draw the conclusion that, in China, carrying out tax cuts is improper and impossible now.

However, no tax cut doesn't mean no role of tax policy in regulating deflation. On the contrary, as one of the most important measures to regulate macroeconomy, taxes always play a part in special fields through a unique mechanism. And then, what shall we do?

First, change the mind and pay attention to institutional innovation of tax policy. In order to deal with deflation, tax policy and tax arrangement based on it must be regulated accordingly. However, considering the regularity of market economy and the specificity of the institutional reform period, it should not follow the traditional thought of solving the problem by strengthening the power of government. Modifying the tax system in response to the changing economic situation with government's economic intervention may be not the advantage of tax policy or the domain it could play a part in. As a normative policy measure, taxation is not a good discretionary policy but a steady measure. As it is emphasized in the case of supporting SOE by funding, it is improper to support SOE with tax cuts but rather by fiscal subsidiaries; for the solution of deflation, tax policy and expenditure policy should focus on different issues. The short-term discretionary matters can be handled by fiscal expenditure policy, and the long-term institutional innovation must be handled by tax policy. It means that tax policy should pay attention to institutional innovation to provide good tax environment for the development of the market economy and steady growth of the national economy.

Second, on condition that existing tax revenue sustains and even increases, the existing tax system should be adjusted partly. It should be noticed that the existing systems in China were formed against the background of a shortage economy and they mainly tend to constrain consumption and depress investment (Li Yang, 1999). So does the tax system. Although there is little space to regulate the aggregates of tax revenue, it is possible to regulate tax revenue partly to stimulate investment and consumption, or at least to avoid depressing investment and consumption demands. If the existing tax system in China is studied carefully, there is much space to do something. For example: shifting the productive added-value tax to a consumptive added-value tax to advance enterprises' ability to upgrade, renovate and expand investment; shifting the business tax levied by real estate sale, construction and installation to added-value tax to reduce enterprises' comparatively heavy investment costs; reducing the consumption tax of those products which were considered luxuries before but are new economic growth points now properly to stimulate consumption demand; unifying the tax systems applied to domestic and foreign enterprises as soon as possible to provide equal environment for all enterprises including SOE; and so on. China's tax system may stride forward to help the development of a market economy and steady economic growth by clearing up the laws, regulations and policies about taxation, as well as the stipulation made by economic sectors and governments at all levels.

Third, bringing the intention of tax cuts into the process of "fee-to-tax" by standardizing government revenue mechanisms. It should be noted that, once we tried hard to complete the task of increasing tax totaling 100 billion Yuan, there was public reflection that the tax burden increased. In this year, especially with the announcement that increase of tax totaling 100 billion Yuan was completed in advance, the complaint about increasing enterprise's tax burden rises. Strictly, the problems happening in these two years are not the result of increasing tax.

Because the existing tax system is not regulated or changed, any action about tightening collection and stopping tax evasion is not carried out in the form of increasing tax, although the result is increased tax revenue. However, enterprises' reference is not the existing system but the past tax burden. For the enterprises, once they pay more tax than ever before, it means tax increases. Therefore, for the enterprises and the real tax they have paid in these two years, the enterprises' tax burden seems to be heavier.

Further, as it is well known, besides normative tax, China's enterprises – especially SOE – have undertaken many nonstandard fees made by governments at all levels. Moreover, the proportion of the latter is larger than the former. In a sense, the reason why government can bear comparatively serious tax evasion is that the revenue of other nonstandard fees can fill up the gap of government expenditure. On condition that enterprises' burden of fees sustains or even increases, any action about tightening collection and avoiding tax evasion (which is of course necessary) will increase enterprises' real tax burden and then increase their total burden. If things go on like this, the increase of investment and consumption demands will be impossible, while SOE reform and development might be more difficult. If enterprises' heavy burden is caused by "heavy fees" but not "heavy tax", the first thing we should do is to start "fee-to-tax" as soon as possible. Moreover, from the macro prospective of standardizing government revenue mechanisms, "fee-to-tax" can be combined with the regulation of the tax system to consider the government revenue and enterprises and residents' burden comprehensively (Gao Peiyong, 1999c). Once government revenue mechanisms have been standardized, enterprises' and residents' burdens will decrease naturally. In another word, the purpose that other countries have to achieve by tax cuts can be realized by standardizing government revenue mechanisms in current China. And its policy effect may be as good as tax cuts.

## References

Central Committee of the Communist Party of China's Decisions About SOE Reform and Development, *Economic Information Daily*, September 27, 1999

Gao Peiyong, 'Fee-to-Tax': the Essence is to Standardize Government Revenue Mechanism, *Economic Daily*, January 25, 1999a

Gao Peiyong, How to Consider China's Current Scale of Treasure Bond, *Economic Loose-Leaf Collection*, Vol.10, 1999b

Gao Peiyong, Promoting Economic Growth: Is Tax Cuts a Choice? *People's Daily*, January 18, 1999c

Huang Da, Enlightenment by Thinking Economic Deflation Calmly – Reviewing the Thoughts About Solving Economic and Financial Problems, *Finance & Trade Economics*, Vol. 8, 1999

Investment Research Group, State Development Planning Commission, Analysis on Current Private Investment, *Economic Loose-Leaf Collection*, Vol.16, 1996

Li Yang, Deflation: Analysis and Countermeasures, *Economic Information Daily*, July 21, 1999

(Originally published in *Economic Research Journal*, Vol.1, 2000)

# 5 Prevention and control of SARS and arrangement of finance and taxation

## Influence and countermeasures

As the unexpected severe acute respiratory syndrome (SARS) impacts China's economic and social development, it also challenges the operation of fiscal revenue and expenditure. In order to deal with this challenge, financial and tax sectors adopted various countermeasures. The objective impact of the SARS epidemic and proactive fiscal and tax countermeasures will influence the situation of fiscal revenue and expenditure this year and for the next few years. Evaluating the influence and plotting corresponding preliminaries are the important things which should be done currently.

For this paper, it should be noted that: first, the main reference is central and local financial budgets in 2003. Various non-normative government revenues and expenditures not covered by budget are not considered. Second, since SARS involves many factors, it is unnecessary and impossible to analyze accurate data in the current situation, so the analysis in this paper is significant to describe general trends.

## Influence of SARS on fiscal revenue

Two clues are important for analyzing the influence of SARS on fiscal revenue. The first one is that the negative influence of SARS on economic growth will be transferred to tax revenue, and it will cause the decrease of fiscal revenue. The other one is that various temporary tax preference measures aiming to deal with the impact of SARS will decrease fiscal revenue directly.

Looking at the first clue: SARS will drag down China's economic growth, and how much it decreases will be decided by the duration of SARS and the control of the illness. However, although there are various uncertain factors, forecasting by authorities and experts at home and abroad pessimistically estimate that economic growth will decease 1–2 percent, and optimistically estimate that economic growth will decrease 0.5–1 percent.[1] That means that the decrease is expected to be in the range of 0.5–2 percent. Regardless which one is accurate, according to the median, economic growth will decrease 1–1.5 percent and the GDP in this year will decrease 100 billion Yuan to 150 billion Yuan. If the proportion of fiscal revenue in GDP is 20 percent this year (it was 18.5 percent last year), it can be estimated that fiscal revenue may decrease 20 billion Yuan to 30 billion Yuan.

Once it involves the structure, things will change again. The industries seriously impacted by SARS include catering service, hotel and hostel, tourism, entertainment, civil aviation, road passenger transportation, waterway passenger transportation, taxi, and so on. All of these industries belong to tertiary industry. The general structure of current tax revenue in China is that the share of turnover tax is 70 percent and the share of income tax is 30 percent. Only one-fourth of turnover tax is business tax. Besides income tax, all the turnover tax paid by tertiary industry is business tax, and only a part of tertiary industry is impacted by SARS. Therefore, the impact on primary and secondary industries is so little that it can be ignored. Because of the current tax system and tax revenue pattern in China, the decrease of fiscal revenue caused by slowed economic growth will be the previously mentioned less than 20 billion Yuan to 30 billion Yuan mentioned.

Then looking at the other clue: so far, the tax funds involved in various tax preferences for coping with SARS can be classified into two forms. The first form is the tax fund derived from SARS. It exempts import tariffs and import linkage value-added taxes on the donated products including protective equipment, diagnostic equipment, therapeutic equipment, monitoring equipment, ambulances, epidemic prevention vehicles and sterilizing carriers which are used to treat and prevent SARS; it exempts individual income tax on special temporary subsidies gained by medical workers who work at the front line of prevention and control of SARS; it also allows deduction of the donation for prevention and control of SARS from income when income tax is calculated. These tax funds appeared and will disappear with SARS. Therefore, the tax preferential policy about them will not cause decrease of the budgetary fiscal revenue. The second form is the existing tax fund. For example, from May 1 to September 30, 2003, exempted were business tax, city maintenance and construction tax, and education surcharges on tourism, civil aviation, catering service, hotels and hostels, taxis, and urban public transportation, and exempted or reduced were individual taxes on taxi drivers. These tax funds are covered by budget and any tax preference about them will decrease the fiscal revenue. However, these kinds of tax preferences only involve a few sources of tax revenue, including business tax and individual tax, and these involved tax categories are not totally free but partly free within five months. Based on the proportion of these tax categories in total tax revenue, it is estimated[2] that the fiscal revenue will decrease 40 billion Yuan to 50 billion Yuan.

Further, the tax revenue has kept rapid growth in these years. From January to April this year, against the background that the impact of SARS appeared preliminarily, the growth rate of tax revenue was 25.8 percent. Besides economic growth, the rapid growth of tax revenue contributes to tightening collection;[3] and in the tide of tightening collection, the decrease of tax revenue might be stopped partly. If the growth rate of tax revenue in this year can keep the same level as last year (12.1 percent), which means it is about 3 percent higher than budgetary growth rate,[4] the decrease of fiscal revenue will be about 50 billion Yuan less than the level previously analyzed.

Considering these factors, it is estimated that the tax revenue will decrease 30 billion Yuan to 40 billion Yuan.

## Influence of SARS on fiscal expenditure

Two clues are important for analyzing the influence of SARS on fiscal expenditure, too. If the measures taken to cope with SARS aim to cure sickness and save patients, as well as to control the epidemic situation, fiscal expenditure will increase – but not greatly. The problem is that the arrangement based on it is decided by the epidemic situation; and from the view of financial sector, it is uncontrollable. This is the first clue. The other clue is that, if the measures taken to cope with SARS exceed the range of prevention and control but aim to increase investment in public health to ensure public health security – which is a long-term consideration – the increase of fiscal expenditure will be significant. Of course, it depends on government choice. Therefore, it is controllable.

So far, governments at all levels have taken various actions to increase fiscal expenditure. For example, the State Council allocates annual total fiscal reserve funds totaling 2 billion Yuan to establish "prevention and control funds allocated by central finance", and it is dedicated to cure patients, purchase medical equipment, pay subsidies to medical workers, reserve drugs and goods, diagnose reagents quickly, and organize research; the provincial, municipal, autonomous regional governments allocate annual local fiscal reserved fund totaled 5 billion Yuan to establish a "Special SARS Prevention and Control Fund" ; the financial sector promises publicly that the medical fees for SARS which can be covered by the public medical system will be paid by the public medical system. For the people who can't enjoy the public medical system, especially farmers and urban poor, they will be cured for free and financial sectors at all levels will pay for them. Even more, besides the medical fee, the other relevant fees such as hospitalization expense and money spent on meals will be paid by the government; the Ministry of Finance decides to support the central civil aviation and tourist enterprises which are seriously impacted by SARS financial discount when it makes a short-term loan, and so on.

Looking at those projects carefully, almost all of these measures which don't exceed the range of prevention and control belong to temporary arrangements. Prevention and control only will cost money, but not much – at least, compared with China's annual fiscal expenditure totaled 2 trillion Yuan, it is so little. Taking Beijing's investment on prevention and control for example, from accepting treatment to leaving hospital, the direct fee spent on a serious SARS patient will be more than 60,000 Yuan, and it will be more than 20,000 Yuan for a mild SARS patient. Even though there are other expenses, if the current epidemic situation doesn't get worse, the money spent on it is estimated to be 10 billion Yuan to 20 billion Yuan.

However, people realize that SARS this time reflects not only weak ability to deal with a public health emergency, but also less investment in the public health system and public health security. It is typical that for many hospitals, especially primary hospitals, the basic care depends on traditional three pieces of equipment: stethoscope, sphygmomanometer and thermometer. In order to build the physical base of the public health system and public health security, government should increase investment in public health by this chance.

Once the view on SARS reaches this level, and the fiscal expenditure is planned on condition of it, there are many things we can do. In order to do these things well, money should be spent. Although the short-term investment can be controlled according to fiscal revenue and expenditure, long-term investment is necessary in spite of great inputs. At least, the investment must increase greatly in the next few years. It must be clear, and the increase of fiscal expenditure caused by it must be analyzed.

Considering the influence of revenue and expenditure together, the primary conclusion can be made that in the short term, SARS will increase budgetary deficit but not much this year, and it can be controlled within the amount of 50 billion Yuan to 60 billion Yuan. In the long term, fiscal expenditure on public health will jump, which press the operation of fiscal revenue and expenditure in the next few years.

## Optional fiscal countermeasures

No matter what perspective it is from, the challenge during the period of SARS is serious for China's finances. For the heavy burden undertaken by China's finances, various countermeasures used to deal with the challenge must look ahead into the future and back into the past. Based on the current situation in China, focus should be on the situation in the future.

In the short term, it seems that deficit can be decreased by the measures below:

### *Using reserve funds*

"Budgetary reserve fund" belongs to budgetary expenditure, the proportion of which in annual fiscal revenue at the same governmental level is about 1–5 percent, and it is mainly used to cope with unexpected emergencies. The total central fiscal budgetary reserve fund may be approved only by the State Council, and is allocated by the Premier her/himself; total fiscal budgetary reserve funds of the government at all levels are controlled by the highest power departments of corresponding government at all levels. At present, central and local finances have allocated reserved funds totaled 2 billion Yuan and 5 billion Yuan, respectively, and they all establish special SARS prevention and control funds. If there is no other important emergency this year, or even if there is emergency this year, so long as the fiscal expenditure is not much, it is possible to increase the usage of reserve funds.

### *Tightening collection*

In recent years, the correlation between increasing tax revenue and tightening collection in China has increased more and more. For example, "two factors" including "economic factor + factor about collection and administration" are used to explain the increase of tax revenue during the period from January to April this year, when the growth rate of tax revenue was 25.8 percent – about 10 percent of it was contributed to economic growth,[5] and the rest, 15 percent, was contributed to collection and administration. By tightening collection, the growth rate of tax revenue could keep at the level above 20 percent, against the background that the influence of SARS on domestic economy appears primarily. Therefore, it is significant for the operation of fiscal revenue and expenditure impacted by SARS to carry out tightening collection further to get the increase of tax revenue beyond budget and weaken the influence of decreased tax revenue.

### Reducing expenditure

Reducing fiscal expenditure is another measure to reduce fiscal deficit. In the last 10 days of April, the Ministry of Finance issued the *Notice about Central Departments to Adjust the Departmental Budget in 2003 to Ensure the Fee about SARS Prevention and Control*, requiring central departments to reduce general public expenditure including conference, traveling and training expenses, and charges abroad, to ensure the availability of money required by SARS prevention and control. In the serious situation created by SARS, so long as central and local governments and departments can try hard to reduce the comparatively high general public expenditure, even it can reduce a few parts of it, the increased fiscal deficit caused by SARS will be improved to some extent.

### Increasing treasury bonds

The government plans to issue treasury bonds totaling 640.4 billion Yuan, including 319.8 billion Yuan to fill up the deficit, 295.6 billion Yuan to pay matured debt, 140 billion Yuan to carry out proactive fiscal policy; and 25 billion Yuan to issue bonds for local government. Since the fiscal deficit may increase because of SARS, even though the usage of reserved fund and tax revenue can reduce partial impact, it needs to cover the rest of the deficit by issuing additional treasury bonds.[6] Comparatively, it is the last line of defense to reduce fiscal deficit impacted by SARS.

In the long term, in order to cope with emergencies like SARS, China must speed up the construction of a public fiscal system. Only if it shifts both the starting point and end of the operation of fiscal revenue and expenditure to satisfy public demand, only if it eliminates the expense of the items which do not belong to or cannot be covered by public demand, only if it puts all the items about the operation of fiscal revenue and expenditure under the supervision and restriction in public, China's finance can build a real emergency mechanism to cope with public health emergencies, and build physical, technical and financial bases to ensure public health security, as well as create fewer detours to play its role well in the event of various emergencies.

(Originally published in *Taxation Research*, Vol. 6, 2003)

## Notes

1 Information from Domestic and Foreign Authorities and Experts' Forecasting about China's Economic Growth, *Economic Information Daily*, May 15, 2003.
2 In 2002, based on total social tax revenue, the proportion of business tax revenue gained from service industry and traffic transportation was 3.9 percent and 1.3 percent, respectively.

3  In the past few years, government and theorists inclined to explain the rapid growth of tax by "three factors" including economic growth, policy regulation and tightening collection. Because no tax policy was issued in the period from January to April of 2003, the growth of tax revenue can only be explained by "two factors".

4  According to different references, there are two methods to calculate growth rate of tax; the first is to compare it with the amount in the previous year, and the other is to compare it to budget.

5  The macroeconomics fundamental principles indicate that the growth rate of tax may be little higher than the economic growth rate.

6  Issuing additional treasury bonds here means to issue additional general treasury bonds to cover deficit. It means that, the writer disapproves of the issuing of "public health treasury bonds" with a fixed sum for a fixed purpose.

# 6 Proactive fiscal policy pursuits for both philosophical and initiative breakthroughs

## Further implementation of proactive fiscal policy is neither simple stereotype nor fine-tuning

Dissension has always existed among people over the issue of whether "proactive" is an appropriate term to describe our fiscal policy, but in recent five-year practical activities, both the official and the academic circles view it as synonymous with expansionary fiscal policy.[1] However, it differs from expansionary fiscal policy in a general sense. By far what we have done under proactive fiscal policy is to increase the issuance of treasury bonds in order to expand fiscal expenditure and then drive domestic demand for the final goal of rapid economic growth. All the time the policy keeps the focus on "increasing issuance of treasury bonds to expand expenditure", so insiders name it as "lame fiscal policy" while outsiders summarize it as "treasury bond policy" or "treasury bond issuance policy".

After the Central Economic Work Conference (CEWC), held at the end of last year, made a significant decision that China would continue to implement proactive fiscal policy, both the 16th National Congress of the Communist Party of China and the First Session of the Tenth National People's Congress (NPC) affirmed the necessity to continue to implement proactive fiscal policy. In addition, in the work plan of the new government, proactive fiscal policy is viewed as the primary means to maintain a rapid economic growth and therefore great importance is attached to it.[2] This at least embodies that – not to mention other meanings – within the recent period, China's economic growth, social stability and other development cannot do without the support of expansionary fiscal policy; and proactive fiscal policy that is keynoted with expanding domestic demand will still be the theme of economic work for the new government.

However, when the policy direction is determined and its implementing measures are being devised, definitely it's widely recognized that continuing to implement proactive fiscal policy cannot and shouldn't be just a simple stereotype or fine-tuning as it was five years ago. Given that China's macroeconomy and its trend have been fundamentally changed, proactive fiscal policy to be further implemented should undergo a structural adjustment based on the last five-year practices over changes.

First, the proactive fiscal policy implemented in the last five years achieved 1.5 percent, 2 percent, 1.7 percent, 1.8 percent and 2 percent economic growth, respectively, but left us some regrets that private consumption and investment were not increased as much as expected. Since the date when proactive fiscal policy was initiated, our objective has always been to stimulate private consumption and investment demand by the fuel of government investment and finally recover the inherent growth order of our economy. However, five years later, it's still the insufficient demand for private consumption and investment that makes us much worried. Government investment alone gets only aggregate economic growth that is directly fueled by external pushes in return. Compared with a considerable amount of continuous government investment, private consumption and investment – specially the former – are not active at all. Therefore, to further implement proactive fiscal policy, we should make material breakthroughs in stimulating private consumption and investment.

Second, the proactive fiscal policy implemented in the last five years has accumulated considerable quality state-owned assets, and also leaves us debts of up to 660 billion Yuan that are credited to the property of proactive fiscal policy and the risk that expanded fiscal expenditure turns into the endogenous prerequisite of economic growth. Debts need payment in the end, let alone those with a nature of proactive fiscal policy which are a component of China's current debts. In addition to national debts used to make up a deficit and those borrowed to pay off old ones, China's accumulated national debt has increased to 20.0824 trillion Yuan by the end of 2002 from 592.88 billion Yuan in 1997,[3] or 18 percent of GDP from 7.93 percent in 1997. With more treasury bonds issued and fiscal expenditure expanded, economic growth relies more on fiscal expenditure expansion, which, to some extent, even evolves into a constant of economic growth. If fast accumulation of national debts and the dependence of economic growth on fiscal expenditure expansion are viewed as the cost of the proactive fiscal policy implemented in the last five years, pursuing more benefits and attempting to digest the current cost after weighing the cost against the benefits will be a significant and inevitable theme when we continue to implement proactive fiscal policy for the purpose of potential risk prevention.

Third, the macroeconomic principles indicate that the stimulation or the pull of fiscal expenditure expansion to the economic growth, even just the direct push on economic aggregate by external fuels, is on the decline. To sustain the original stimulation or pull, fiscal expenditure has to keep expanding on its previous scale; while to enhance the original stimulation or pull, fiscal expenditure has to expand on a larger scale. When a proactive fiscal policy has been implemented for five consecutive years, sustaining the original scales of extra treasury bond issuance and fiscal expenditure expansion will not be as effective as before, even though the so-called fading-out strategy is not applied. To follow the operation mode in the last five years and keep that stimulation or pull, it has to increase the dosage – issuing more treasury bonds and further expanding fiscal expenditure. In that case, it would increase the potential risks of fiscal mechanisms, even overall economic and social risks, not to mention the sustainability of fiscal balance.

Fourth, compared with the last five years, especially in 1998 when proactive fiscal policy was first implemented, today's macroeconomy has already gone through tremendous changes. Insufficient demand and economic downturn are still our principal contradictions, and the momentum effect of deflation still works, but we are on the rise from the bottom. With global economic upturn, China's national economy will – if not, surprisingly – be expected to transition from recession to blossoming at the end of this year or the early part of next year, unless unexpected incidents occur. Providing solid evidence are positive CPI growth and economy growth rate up to 9.9 percent in this first quarter, even 8.9 percent in this April when SARS raged. Therefore, keeping anti-deflation while preventing inflation, expanding domestic demand while fading out, should be the unique feature that distinguishes the proactive fiscal policy to be further implemented from what it was like in the last five years.

We will see many new characteristics for certain if we continue to implement proactive fiscal policy. We need to discuss and understand these characteristics before outlining a blueprint about how we continue to implement proactive fiscal policy. It should be one of our research focuses on China's macroeconomic policy.

For the convenience of discussion, this paper quotes "to continue to implement proactive fiscal policy" and discusses what it will do next.

## Reforms promote economic growth: new thoughts about how to continue to implement proactive fiscal policy

Speaking of what the proactive fiscal policy has achieved in the last five years, the first coming to mind is a series of proud achievements that the treasury bond investment has made in infrastructure construction and its direct contribution to economic growth. For example, water conservancy, eco-environment, transportation, urban infrastructure and rural grid reconstruction have been developed very quickly in the last few years and pulled economic growth significantly.[4] No doubt it's the primary functioning mode of proactive fiscal policy, but not the exclusive mode. Apart from expanding investment demand, there are also many measures to foster and expand consumption demand. For example, in order to increase incomes of urban and rural low- and middle-income residents, since 1999, salary benchmark and pensions for nationwide public institutions have been raised on a large scale for three consecutive years, the year-end bonus mechanism has been carried out, and allowances for employees working in remote areas have been set up; benefits for retirees of state-owned enterprises have been raised; the social security system has been improved, and incomes and subsidies of urban and rural low-income residents have been increased; and many reforms have been initiated to increase rural income, such as returning farmlands to forests and deepening reformation of rural taxation system and food circulation system.

In the last five years, urban and rural residents increased their income significantly in a large amount and a large margin. Per capita salary in public institutions was even doubled. From a wider scale, per capita disposable income of urban families increased to 7703 Yuan in 2002 from 5160 Yuan in 1997, or by 8.6 percent per year; per capita net income of rural families increased to 2476 Yuan in 2002 from 2090 Yuan in 1997, or by 3.8 percent per year.[5]

However, it's known to all that the increased urban and rural income does not drive consumption demand to rise, but becomes the direct stimulator to a fast deposit growth. Urban and rural RMB deposit balances kept a linear growth from 4.6 trillion Yuan in 1997 to 8.7 trillion Yuan in 2002, and even stepped over 10 trillion Yuan and reached the record level of 10.2 trillion Yuan in this April. With stocks, securities and other financial assets also held in their hands, it's more obvious that residents prefer those to savings. Moreover, the comparison between income increase and deposit increase in the last few years shows that, apart from the increased disposable income of urban and rural residents, their excessive savings – those increased by economizing consumption – are also a large contribution to the saving increment. For example, last year, the deposit balance of urban and rural residents increased 17.8 percent over the previous year, but per capita disposable income increased by only 10 percent in the same period.[6] The two have a gap of 7.8 percentage points.

A variety of measures to stimulate consumption demand is not as effective as infrastructure investment, to say the least. And to a large extent, the reason that we have to continue to implement proactive fiscal policy under the heavy fiscal burden and greater potential risks is the insufficient consumption demand (Lu Wei, 2003). It can't be denied that it's a defect of proactive fiscal policy.

But the problem is determining what causes this defect.

By far, economic academic circles' studies on urban and rural income distribution and consumer psychology have shown two facts, as follows:

First, although urban and rural income has a large increase in its aggregate and rapid growth, its distribution is always structurally imbalanced – and even more now. Take Gini coefficient for example, a statistical measure of the degree of variation represented in a set of values. The year of 2000 saw the national disposable income with a Gini coefficient of 0.458, 12.8 percentage points higher than the year of 1979 at the beginning of the reform, and already above 0.4, the internationally accepted alarm level; the urban and rural income gap enlarged from 2.79 times in 2000, to 2.91 times in 2001 and up to 3 times in 2002; as for the upper- and lower- income tiers, per capita disposable income gap between the 10 percent upper- and 10 percent lower-income tiers was 4.62 times in 1999.[7] Hence it's not difficult to understand China's urban and rural depositor composition: small- and medium-sized depositors making up 80 percent of total depositors contributed to 40 percent of total deposits while the upper-income tier making up 20 percent of total depositors contributed to 60 percent of total deposits. Currency income is concentrated towards the minorities. The upper- and lower-income tiers, and the urban and rural residents, have great differences in margin consumption tendency. As a result, people who have much consumption demand have little money, while those who have little demand have much money. How can such structural imbalance between income distribution and consumption demand not lead to decreased total consumption of urban and rural residents? Under such circumstances, consumption demand tells its own tale of changes.

Second, although their incomes are on the rise, people see frequent changes of all systems related to their livelihood and anticipate more and more expenditures now and in the future: houses go to the commercial market, so people have to divide a part of their incomes to pay a housing mortgage after they buy a house; children's education is paid by their parents, who have to save more money for their children to receive better and higher education, or even more modern education overseas; not all medical expenses are paid by the government – the proportion undertaken by individuals keeps increasing, and what's going on in the future is unknown; and pension amount is a very small fraction of the employment compensation, so people who are about to retire have to make plans against the rainy days, and now there are no explicit regulations on how much pension they could get and how they could get it in the future. At the same time, quite a few people underestimate their future incomes. Indefinite prospective income and expenditure and the Chinese tradition of prudence are the reasons why people – no matter the rich or the poor during the reform period – dare not to spend at will or feel free to spend, but are inclined to prudent spending.

Those two facts tell us that the unreasonable income distribution system and uncertain institutional expectations are probably the primary reasons why the government confronts frustration over and over again in pulling consumption demand. The two also inspire us in today's China: the fundamental way out of stimulating consumption demand and promoting domestic demand is to accelerate the reform process and set up an institutional base for the market economy. Once the income distribution relation is clear and the income distribution system adapts to institutional environment of market economy, income distribution and consumption demand will be structurally balanced and total consumption of urban and rural residents will tend to be reasonable and increased. Once the future institutional framework is clear and the income and expenditure expectation is definite, people will feel free to spend reasonably.

In fact, the rule applicable to driving consumption demand also applies to realizing other policy objectives, doesn't it? Since China's reform has gained today's achievements, nothing will take more effects but further deepening the reform, shortening the transition from the old system to a new one, and implementing macroeconomic policies such as proactive fiscal policy based on a market economy.

The importance of reform to economic growth can be demonstrated by the institutional economics and Chinese experience. One of the statements of institutional economics is that institutional transformation is the power and source of economic growth, and much more important to economic growth than material capital, human capital, labors and technologies. China's economic miracles gained in the last 20 years are directly correlated with the process of the reform and opening up. Again, the findings of quantitative analysis prove from different aspects that the institutional variables such as "non state-owned level", "marketization" and "openness" since the reform have had significant effects on China's rapid economic growth (Renmin University of China, 2003). In other words, institutional transformation is the core factor of our high-speed economic growth.

When we explore the essential conditions for accelerating and deepening the reform from the perspective of "reform-driven growth", we surprisingly find out that Chinese fiscal policy has not only made contributions in "paving the way" but accumulated successful experience during that process over the last 20 years when the marketization reform was advanced.

An outstanding example happened at the beginning of the reform. We know China's economic system reform started from the distribution sector and the first keynote was "decentralization of power and transfer of profits". But during that period, the power to be decentralized was the fiscal administration and the profits to be transferred actually referred to the fiscal ratio of national income distribution. No matter decentralization of power – for example, dividing central and local governments apart by starting from reforming fiscal administration systems to adjusting public revenue distribution between central and local governments, or transfer of profits – for example, a large scale of tax reduction and a variety of subsidies for enterprises and residents, were actually to encourage various reforms and create favorable conditions for introducing reform initiatives at the cost of public revenue reduction and expenditure increase.

The "paving the way" role of finance is branded at the crucial stage of the reform and even in the path to institutional innovation. Examples are summarized from the "tax for profits" reform milestone, to the establishment of the foreign taxation system and new accounting system as propellers; from 1994 fiscal and tax reform with the focus on income alone to the overall fiscal institutional transformation on both income and expenditure; from starting "fee-to-tax" and "tax and fee reform" aiming at regulating public revenue and government institutions, to building a framework of a public fiscal system adaptive to the market economy. Generally speaking, exchanging fiscal imbalance and reform for the success of overall economic system transformation is by far a retroactive clue of China's market-oriented reform (Gao Peiyong and Wen Laicheng, 2001).

On the one hand, reform provides inexhaustible impetus and source for sustainable and fast economic growth; on the other hand, it's always a tradition for China's finance to "pave the way" for starting and advancing reforms. When our analysis is extended to such a level, the relation between the proactive fiscal policy to be further implemented and all proposed reforms or those about to be implemented and their potential effects seems to unfold. Following the historic path that proactive fiscal policy was implemented to "increase issuance of treasury bonds for expenditure expansion", the investment of revenue from additional treasury bonds or the arrangements for expenditure expansion shall be combined with all proposed reforms or those about to be implemented. In that way, the former could pave the way for successful introduction or objective setting of the latter, breaking the boundary of the historic path and maneuvering as many fiscal elements as possible in order to implement proactive fiscal policy. Adjusting either public revenue or expenditure, or inter-linking both, shall be combined with all proposed reform initiatives or those about to be implemented, and shall also pave the way for their successful introduction or objective setting.

A conclusion is reached after so many discussions that we should and have to break free from our conventional thoughts if we continue to implement proactive fiscal policy. We need to continue to stimulate demand directly by "increasing issuance of national debts to expand expenditure". Furthermore, we need to – at an appropriate time – take the road of "promoting economic growth with reforms", such that our focus is to lay a solid foundation for our reform acceleration and deepening, and to establish an institutional base for sustainable rapid growth of our economy. We should attach significant importance to fueling domestic demand by expanding expenditure and promoting marketization reform by intensifying fiscal elements, as well. They reflect our expectations on both short- and long-term effects. They are well coordinated to drive sustainable rapid growth of our economy. Their combination may be another big breakthrough about how we continue to implement proactive fiscal policy at the conceptual level.

This doesn't mean we return to the road of "paying for the reform" but combine the practices of proactive fiscal policy with the institutional transformation of our national economy together under the banner of institutional innovation, so as to pursue sustainable rapid growth of economy.

This doesn't mean we have to make a fresh start when we continue to implement proactive fiscal policy, but need to align proactive fiscal policy with economic institutional transformation according to our updated thoughts and dynamic economic conditions. The former reflects our short-term objective to expand domestic demand, while the latter reflects our long-term objective to build an institutional base for a market economy. We need to explore strategies for sustainable rapid economic growth on the chessboard of economy and society.

By the way, through such arrangements probably we would receive a theoretical "windfall", breaking the debate on the definition of "proactive" fiscal policy. As mentioned before, we selected "proactive" fiscal policy spoken for expansionary fiscal policy out of political wisdom against a special background. When "proactive" equals "expansionary", the doubt rises whether there is "passive" fiscal policy, as people assume that "passive" means "tight". When proactive fiscal policy is always embodied by actively promoting reforms, actively committing to sustainable rapid economic growth and actively intervening macroeconomic regulation, expansionary fiscal policy for expanding demand and tight fiscal policy for tightening demand should get back to their proper positions.

## Revenue and expenditure measures undertaken concurrently: new initiatives are required for further implementation of proactive fiscal policy

No doubt, breaking the boundary of conventional thoughts leads to dramatic changes of the initiatives and new thoughts are realized through new initiative arrangements.

One of the new thoughts is that we should keep abreast of "stimulating domestic demand" and "promoting marketization reform". It's noted that this new thought should be carried out on the basis that proactive fiscal policy is implemented with as many fiscal elements as possible. Hence, we can no longer concern only fiscal expenditure but ignore public revenue – especially do nothing or do a little in tax collection. Instead, we should set up a new pattern that expenditure and revenue measures are taken concurrently and coordinated.

The clues discussed previously tell us that, apart from those conventional and widely accepted measures, the new initiatives for us to continue to implement proactive fiscal policy in present China include at least the following:

The first goes to tax system adjustment. History tells us that the tax system in any country should be rooted in its economic and social environment and adjusted to its changes. The prevailing tax system in China, designed in 1993 and implemented since the next year, has been developed for 10 years. During this period, its fundamental pattern almost stays the same despite some small revisions and modifications. By contrast, China's economic and social environment has gone through tremendous changes in the same period, so the tax system becomes increasingly unmatched with its root, the economic and social environment of today's China. It's also recognized that the tax system will have negative impacts on economic development unless its adjustment keeps pace with the times. For example, the present tax system was born in shortage economy and branded with disinflation. Now its effect deviates far from our macroeconomic objectives in the current period when the shortage economy disappears and counter-deflation outweighs anything.

Although theorists and functional departments have done much research and even produced feasible practical solutions, too much is said and too little is done actually regarding the tax system adjustment. The primary reason goes to the wide worries about reduction or declined growth of tax revenue. The established VAT adjustment solution aims at transformation[8] and the tax revenue is estimated to decrease 80 billion Yuan, 50 billion Yuan and 30 billion Yuan, respectively, under major, medium and minor adjustment. Such a large decline of our tight finance frightens the policy makers from moving forward. Adjustment on corporate income tax, individual income tax, consumption tax and others failed to appear on the agenda due to the same or similar reasons. The tax authority once suggested a conception of "structural adjustment with both increase and decrease" (Jin Renqing, 2002), which means that the total tax revenue stays almost the same through some increases and some decreases. To optimize the tax system, there must be a transition from adjustment and implementation to final goal attainment. During the transition period, fluctuated tax revenue is quite possible, which is bound to hinder policy making.

The problem is that it cannot go on for long to put aside the tax system adjustment that is proposed or about to be carried out due to the worries about public revenue reduction. If the tax system was not adjusted until our finances were much relieved, the adjustment would be at a far distant date and it would do more harm than good at the macroscopic level when slowed-down economic development is considered. Hence on the chessboard about how to continue to implement proactive fiscal policy, a position must be reserved for tax system adjustment.

The second goes to the reform of social security system. Among China's reforms in every aspect, the reform of social security system already becomes a bottleneck. Its success, to some extent, determines those reforms on state-owned enterprises, rural areas, finance, employment and re-employment, so people are clearly aware of the significance of the reform of the social security system. We cannot deny that the updated solutions for the reform of social security system are somewhat feasible.

But the reform of social security system, especially attainment of its objectives, costs considerably. As an important sector of social public demand, a social security system beneficial to all members of society should be established with the push of government, and its operation should rely on the public revenue and expenditure system. If it was done, the government would have to bear more responsibilities and pay more costs than now. Conclusively, the government has to spend more than it does now on reform of the social security system. In fact, our severely insufficient funding results in a slower reform process and underestimated reform objectives. We can hardly even maintain the lowest level of the social security fund as promised before.

If finances are the primary reason to hinder the reform of social security system, it does make sense that we should make some efforts to promote the reform of the social security system and spend some funds to raise its objectives to an upper level when we continue to carry out proactive fiscal policy.

The third goes to rural reform. Among the four reforms that the new government plans to carry out, the rural reform is the first priority. Premier Wen Jiabao stated five challenges in a press conference, and the first was underdeveloped agriculture and the slow increase of rural income. The severity of the Three Rural Issues (agriculture, rural areas and farmers) and the importance of rural reforms at present are quite self-evident.

There is always a huge gap between urban and rural areas in China, which once narrowed down at the early of the reform for a while and began to widen again in recent years. The farmers account for 64 percent of total pollution, but their per capita disposable income is below that of the urban residents.[9] They have to pay more taxes and fees than urban residents but are treated very unfairly; for example, they are unable to get the same public commodities or services as the urban residents (Yang Bin, 2002). Long before today people have come to recognize such gaps and their potential dangers. To narrow down or eliminate some gaps is not objectively impossible. The good example is what people usually talk about, the so-called "two 30 billion Yuan", namely, the agriculture taxes and the compulsory education fees exclusively collected from the farmers are each 30 billion Yuan per year. No matter from which point of view, giving national treatment to farmers and solving the Three Rural Issues are what the government should and must do as soon as possible. Exempting the two extra burdens for the farmers means 30 billion Yuan less revenue, plus 30 billion Yuan more expenditure for the government. Where can we find out sources to recover this combined fiscal cost of 60 billion Yuan? If nowhere, the financial constraint would stay unchanged and the government would hesitate to make final resolution.

As the Three Rural Issues now become the primary factor to hinder expanding domestic demand and threaten economic growth, fulfilling the goal of building a moderately prosperous society in all respects is heavily dependent on whether the farmers live a well-off life, so rural reform must be one of the indispensable arrangements when we continue to implement proactive fiscal policy.

The fourth goes to tax and fee reform. The tax and fee reform was earlier known as the tax-for-fee reform (TFR). The reason to enact the TFR was that, local governments at all levels charged fees and collected funds from enterprises and residents and spent these fees without prior permission of finance and tax authorities. It disturbed the economic order and levied unbearable burdens on enterprises and residents. To avoid total government revenue out of control due to "corresponding adjustment", the tax and fee reform was later proposed that taxes replacing excessive fees should be included into local government revenue and should be expended under the plan of local governments. Either the earlier TFR or the tax and fee reform later, it's intended to regulate local government behaviors and the mechanism in terms of revenue and expenditure, and then establish a public fiscal system adaptive to the market economy. Some studies have already shown that this move has cut off the administrative departments' hands to grab illegal income from enterprises and residents, because it microscopically sets clear definitions on current accounts between local governments and enterprises and/or residents, and it also has created favorable conditions to boost enterprise investment and resident consumption. Macroscopically, it involves defining the role of local government and transforming local government functions and has created a legislative environment for the survival and long-term development of enterprises and residents by bringing all local government activities including government revenue and expenditure onto the legal track.

For similar reasons, the tax and fee reform will cut the vested interests of government agencies at all levels and adjust their functions and corresponding fiscal arrangements. As a result, the state finance authorities have to divert a part of normative public revenue to cover these losses of local governments. For example, to initiate the tax and fee reform in rural areas of some provinces, the state revenue has contributed almost 100 billion Yuan in recent years. It's the financial fund that restrains the development of the tax and fee reform, which has not yet gained any fundamental achievement since its official start five years ago. Normative budgetary and non-normative non-budgetary and even non-institutional revenue and expenditures still exist side by side, and the non-normative public revenue and expenditure accounts for a very large proportion.

In such cases, to fulfill the fundamental goals of the tax and fee reform, the public finance has to pay the price, which cannot be spared anytime. It's inevitable to put the tax and fee reform on the agenda when we continue to implement proactive fiscal policy.

There are many other such arrangements that intend to decrease public revenue, or increase fiscal expenditure, or redirect national bond investments, or give up some vested interests. In short, they are exchanged or promoted by financial cost or operation of public revenue and expenditure. It's perhaps not easy – even too hard – to achieve obvious results in the short term. Considering the fact that promoting domestic demand and reform could guarantee the sustainable rapid growth of China's economy, it deserves great efforts right now.

By the way, if such arrangements squeeze out those expensive programs that shouldn't be done, or could be spared, or are done for nothing, China's public revenue system would accelerate its establishment and the effects of the proactive fiscal policy to be continued would be further magnified.

(Originally published in *Finance & Trade Economics*, Vol. 7, 2003)

## Notes

1 Xiang Huaicheng (2002), the former Finance Minister, once used "political wisdom" to illustrate how proactive fiscal policy was conceived: a moderately tight fiscal policy was just determined in the Fifteenth CPC National Congress convened in 1997, but not long after that an expansionary fiscal policy was carried out in fact. Such a change might be unacceptable; hence the wording, a so-called proactive fiscal policy with intent to expand domestic demand, was finally adopted and prevailed.
2 Premier Wen Jiabao said during a press conference on March 18, 2013: "I once concluded the future work into four sentences. The first is to achieve one goal, namely maintaining a rapid economic growth. To achieve that goal, we need to keep the policies stable and constant, adhere to the guideline of expanding domestic demand and implement proactive fiscal policy and prudent monetary policy" (see Economic Information Daily, March 19, 2003).
3 Figures are calculated on previous figures and those in Xiang Huaicheng's (2003) *Reports On 2002 Central and Local Budget Performance and 2002 Central and Local Budget Draft.* The data is 270 billion Yuan more than officially recognized 1.8124 trillion Yuan primarily due to 270 billion Yuan treasury bonds exclusively issued to state-owned commercial banks to supplement their capital funds. It seems to be an account adjustment, but actually it's a part of public debts and should be recorded into the public debts.
4 Cong Ming (2003) finds out 660 billion Yuan of long-term construction national bonds issued from 1998–2002 contributed to the total investment of 3.28 trillion Yuan; and by the end of 2002, the accumulated investments amounted to 2.46 trillion Yuan. During the same period, China's economic growth rate was 7.8 percent, 7.1 percent, 8 percent, 7.3 percent and 8 percent, respectively, and public debt investment contributed to 1.5 percent, 2 percent, 1.7 percent, 1.8 percent and 2 percent, respectively, of the economic growth.
5 From Zhu Rongji's Government Work Report, *People's Daily*, March 20, 2003.
6 From Liu Sheng's Why Common People Are Reluctant to Spend, *China Taxation News*, April 25, 2003.
7 From Sun Liping's *Polarization: Two Impetuses of Market and Power,* Inside Information of Economic Reform, Vol.19, 2001.
8 This means to transform the production-type VAT to a consumption-type VAT, deduct the taxes recorded into fixed assets and relieve heavy investment burden for enterprises. For more about tax reform, please see the author's *Passive and Active Adjustments on China's Taxation System after WTO*, International Economic Review, vol. 11–12, 2002.
9 Statistics show that in the most recent five years the urban per capita income increased 8.6 percent per year while the rural increased only 3.8 percent (the former is 2.6 times of the latter). Economic Monthly, Vol.4, 2003, p. 29.

## References

Cong Ming, Assessment on China's Economic and Fiscal Policies and Financial Risks, *China's Economic and Social Forum, China's Association of Economy and Society*, Vol.2, February 2003

Gao Peiyong and Wen Laicheng, *China's Public Finance Operating Mechanism in Marketization Process*, China Renmin University Press, 2001

Jin Renqing, *Comments on Chinese Contemporary Tax Revenue*, People's Publishing House, 2002

Lu Wei, Consumption Impedes Proactive Fiscal Policy, *Economic Information Daily*, April 3, 2003

Renmin University of China, *Research Report on 2002 China's Economic Development*, China Renmin University Press, 2003

Xiang Huaicheng, Proactive Fiscal Policy Is Political Wisdom, *China Times*, August 17, 2002

Xiang Huaicheng, Reports on 2002 Central and Local Budget Performance and 2002 Central and Local Budget Draft, *China State Finance*, Vol. 4, 2003

Yang Bin, *China's Three Rural Issues After Its Entry Into WTO*, What the Economists Say About China After Its Entry Into WTO, Economic Science Press, 2002

# 7 Icebreaking prudent fiscal policy

## Analysis of the current orientation of China's fiscal policy

### Preface

Since the second half of 2003 when the economy entered a new expansionary process, China's economic circles including the macroeconomic control administrations had an extraordinarily heated debate on the orientation adjustment of fiscal policy. This debate lasted for about 18 months and ended at the end of 2004 when prudent fiscal policy was finally determined at the Central Economic Work Conference (CEWC).

This debate went through three phases. in chronologic order:

The first phase started in June 2003 when the economy got over SARS and returned to the track of strong growth, and ended at the end of November when the CEWC made the decision that we should continue to implement proactive fiscal policy. Subjects discussed during this phase included: Is the economy overheated? Is it partially or completely heated? Is it the time for the proactive fiscal policy implemented for over six years to fade out or exit as the macroeconomy changes?

The second phase started at the end of November when the CEWC came to a close and the economy – especially investment – was extremely overheated and ended in May 2004 when Finance Minister Jin Renqing announced at the Global Conference on Poverty Reduction that the orientation of our fiscal policy was shifted from proactive to neutral. Subjects discussed during this phase included: How can fiscal policy be always well functioning amid instantaneous changes as a discretionary macro-control approach? Is it possible to have "inverse regulation" effects if we continue to implement proactive fiscal policy? What on earth hinders the fiscal policy adjustment? When and under what conditions is such adjustment necessary?

The third phase started in May 2004 when neutral fiscal policy was proposed and ended at the beginning of December when the CEWC decided to shift to prudent fiscal policy. Subjects discussed during this phase included: Is it appropriate to quote neutral fiscal policy? How do we understand its connotation and denotation? Is it better to fade out or quit from the expansionary track, or just to shift immediately to a tight policy? What's the relationship between neutral fiscal policy and tight monetary policy? How far can neutral fiscal policy go in reality?

Finally, the proactive fiscal policy lasting for almost seven years officially dropped its curtain, and discussions on fiscal policy orientation were also settled down.

Seemingly, macroeconomic changes are the impetus for the extended discussions on fiscal policy orientation, but the discussions are just based on stereotypes of the previous ones. Once macroeconomic conditions encounter a periodic change, macroeconomic policies need to adapt themselves correspondingly and the question "where the fiscal policy heads to" will be raised again. Similar discussions won't stop until macroeconomic conditions have no more periodic changes. In essence, in this heated debate during the period of Chinese economic transformation, the hard decision-making and the complex process together reflect and highlight many new factors and features that we have never ever met and will emerge again when similar macroeconomic conditions and policy adjustment repeat themselves in the future. These new factors and features will even become significantly decisive factors in deciding macroeconomic policies.

The review of this zigzag debate and decision-making reveals these new and highlighted factors and features. Based on that, it is quite necessary for us to summarize and extract the changing rules and select macro-control measures before we understand the current macroeconomic decision-making – and study the future trend, as well. Moreover, it's favorable to enrich China's fiscal macro-control theories and improve its craftsmanship.

Those mentioned tasks make up the subjects of this paper.

## Basic practices of proactive fiscal policy

As the proactive fiscal policy lasted for seven years from 1998 to the end of 2004, no further analysis will be completed in this paper unless the practices throughout that period are introduced first in detail.

### Policy connotation

People hold dissenting opinions whether "proactive" accurately defines the fiscal policy that was implemented throughout the last seven years in their practical activities; nevertheless, both officials and academics agree about the proactive policy being equivalent to an expansionary one. The former Finance Minister Xiang Huaicheng (2002a) once used "political wisdom" to illustrate the background of introducing proactive fiscal policy: moderately tight fiscal policy was just determined in the Fifteenth CPC (Communist Party of China) National Congress in 1997 and the first session of the Ninth NPC in March 1998, but not long after that an expansionary policy was implemented in fact. As people might be unable to accept this change, the so-called proactive fiscal policy finally prevailed with the intention of expanding domestic demand. Hence, the proactive policy is actually the synonym of expansionary policy as far as its connotation is concerned.

### Policy content

The proactive fiscal policy changes its measures or shifts its focus every year throughout its seven-year practice. For example, it's the additional volume of long-term construction treasury bonds that is the primary measure to increase infrastructure investment at the beginning, but later it extends to every aspect like the technical upgrading for state-owned enterprises (SOEs), the raise of the minimum living level of urban low-income residents and the salaries for civil servants, and the cessation of the fixed asset investment regulatory tax. Its basic content is to conclusively increase construction treasury bond issuance to expand fiscal expenditure and then drive domestic demand in order to achieve the final goal of rapid economic growth. Hence, the proactive policy is summarized as "bond issuance increase and expenditure expansion" as far as its content is concerned.

### Policy effects

The effects of the seven-year proactive fiscal policy cover many aspects. For example, important infrastructure construction is enhanced, industrial structure adjustment is promoted, regional productive resources are re-allocated, investment environment is improved, and the SOE reform is supported; but generally speaking, its fundamental effect is the stimulus on national economic growth. The policy efficacy concentrates on the stimulus on domestic demand and then the GDP growth. Quantitative analysis determines that the proactive policy has boosted 1–2 percentage points of GDP growth rate per year (Cong Ming, 2003; Jin Renqing, 2004b).

### Policy costs

Everything has its own benefits and costs. During those seven years when proactive fiscal policy was implemented, what was achieved cost us too much. Apart from the costs in other aspects, only the figures on the scale of national debts and relevant indices cannot be neglected. They are: (1) 910 billion Yuan of the accumulated volume of long-term construction treasury bonds issued (Figure 7.1); (2) 270 billion Yuan of special treasury bonds issued as a supplement to capital

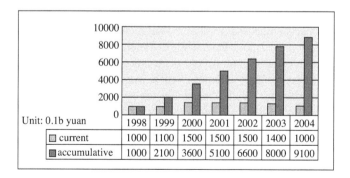

*Figure 7.1* The Current and Accumulated Volume of Long-Term Construction Treasury Bonds Issued (1998–2004)

Sources: General Affairs Department, Ministry of Finance: *1991–2004 National Debts*, hard copy, 2004; Ministry of Finance: *Reports on 2004 Central and Local Budget Performance and 2005 Central and Local Budget Draft*, China Securities Journal, March 16, 2005

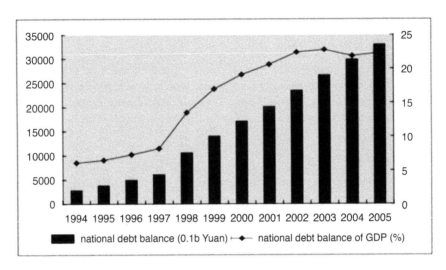

*Figure 7.2* National Debt Balance and Balance-to-GDP Ratio

Sources: General Affairs Department, Ministry of Finance: *1991–2004 National Debts*, hard copy, 2004; Ministry of Finance: *Reports on 2004 Central and Local Budget Performance and 2005 Central and Local Budget Draft*, China Securities Journal, March 16, 2005.

funds of state-owned commercial banks; (3) up to 2.9833 trillion Yuan of national debt balance, well above 607.451 billion Yuan at the end of 1997 (Figure 7.2); and (4) up to 21.9 percent of the debt-to-GDP ratio, well above 8.2 percent at the end of 1997 (General Office, Ministry of Finance, 2004; Ministry of Finance, 2004). These figures would increase sharply if outstanding government debts beyond budget or contingent debts were included (Wang Bao'an, 2004).

## Second-best in the two-choice dilemma: 2004 fiscal policy orientation

In China, both academics and officials are quite familiar with the macroeconomic rationale: inflation needs to deflate, while deflation needs to expand. Fiscal policy, as one of the two macroeconomic control measures, cannot be functional unless it takes tight or expansionary counter-cyclical actions on public revenue. This is common sense known to all, but when they are applied into practical activities, it turns out that it's not easy to determine the fiscal policy orientation in China where proactive fiscal policy has already been carried out for seven years.

In fact, before the CEWC convened at the end of 2003 when proactive fiscal policy came to its sixth year, policy makers overcame considerable difficulties to set the keynote of fiscal policy in the next year, as the cold macroeconomic environment began to get warm. The reason was that, they were not sure whether the economic situation then was "hot" or "cold"; even when they finally reached an agreement, they still found themselves in a dilemma whether to quit or to continue the proactive fiscal policy (Gao Peiyong, 2003a).

### To quit

When macroeconomic situations are believed to get "overheated", proactive fiscal policy, based on "bond issuance increase + expenditure expansion", should brake and "quit in good time". In that case, a series of contradictions that were buried deep down at the bottom probably come to the surface.

In the past six years, local governments made use of revenue from long-term construction treasury bonds issued by the central government and those support-ing funds from their own and local banks to construct many important projects. Some projects are completed, but some still under process. The follow-up funds to complete those in process are estimated to be roughly in the range of 800 bil-lion to 1 trillion Yuan, even without any new projects. If the proactive policy were halted, it would cut the available sources of follow-up funds for projects in process and those projects would be likely to stay abandoned or half-done. This is the first contradiction.

In the past five years, the proactive policy achieved an economic growth rate of 1.5, 2, 1.7, 1.8 and 2 percentage points, respectively. This is the positive argument that we always hold. Our negative argument is that, the GDP growth would have decreased at least 11 percentage points without the fuel of the proactive policy. In other words, when economic growth is already heavily dependent on fiscal expen-diture expansion, to quit the proactive policy will cost us an economic growth of at least 1–2 percentage points per year. This is the second contradiction.

In the past six years, a byproduct resulted from the implementation process of the proactive policy that some regions, industries, authorities and groups were flourishing and withering at the same pace as the proactive policy did. The vested interests of those specific regions, industries, authorities and groups are dependent on the policy sustainability, so the pattern of invested interests will be broken when the policy ends. Stakeholders will surely stand in the way to protect their vested interests[1]; moreover, the accompanying social instabilities will threaten the steady economic and social development to some extent. This is the third contradiction.

### To continue

When macroeconomic situations are believed to stay "overcool" rather than get-ting "overheated", it's quite necessary to continue to implement proactive fiscal policy, but contradictions cannot be ignored.

By the end of 2003, the proactive policy lasting for six years had already left us up to 800 billion Yuan of debts (long-term construction treasury bonds). In addition to those to make up the deficit and those to pay the old debts, China's overall public debts amounted to 2.6635 trillion Yuan, or 22.8 percent of GDP. To continue the proactive policy will undoubtedly enlarge the existing debt scale and increase the debt-to-GDP ratio. The resulting fiscal risks and other risks can hardly be avoided. This is the first contradiction.

Through the six-year activities of the proactive policy, expansionary fiscal expenditure has already evolved into an indispensable endogenous condition of further economic growth. In fact, economic growth becomes more and more dependent on the proactive policy due to the diminishing marginal effect. If we continue the operation mode of "bond issuance increase + expenditure expansion", it indeed fuels economic growth but also enhances its growth dependency on fiscal expenditure expansion. If things go on like this, the results are self-evident. This is the second contradiction.

The longer the proactive policy lasts, the more the accompanying pattern of vested interests is reinforced. To continue the proactive policy means to bring more interests to related regions, industries, authorities and groups in order to get temporary stability in return, but also means the pattern of vested interests will last and become inflexible. However, when various conditions for sustaining the operation mode of "bond issuance increase + expenditure expansion" disappear in the future, instabilities resulting from the broken pattern of vested interests will definitely imperil the stable development of economy and society. This is the third contradiction.

### Enlightenment from the dilemma

To quit or to continue? Neither is the best. When determining the fiscal policy orientation in such a dilemma, it's crucial to find out the room for fiscal policy and keep it in alignment with macroeconomic policies. Gratefully, everything has its pros and cons. Sometimes we are even inspired by something unusual in an adverse condition, something we could hardly get in a favorable condition.

First, the previous actions under the proactive policy have made astonishing achievements – but also left us some regrets. For example, government investment alone doesn't lead to private consumption demand as active as expected, but pays a high cost in that both soaring national debts and economic growth become heavily dependent on fiscal expenditure expansion. This enlightens us that we need to adjust our current orientation of the proactive policy that used to cost much but be inefficient, if we'd like to keep our focus on demand stimulus.

Second, in the first 20 years of this century – a very important strategic period – the national economy has to keep growth above 7.2 percent per year to quadruple GDP and to build a well-off society in an all-round way. Besides, China also needs to seize opportunities out of economic growth to create more jobs and adjust its economic structure. Although the importance of economic growth is relatively lessened by the rise of the new concept of harmonious development of both economy and society, we still have to pursue higher economic growth in order to cover our history bills, the outcome of our partial focus on economic growth in the past. Whereas government investment is still an important driving force for China's economic growth, and China's economic growth cannot do without fiscal expenditure expansion, fiscal policy has to commit itself to demand expansion in the short term.

Third, a considerable amount of money is needed to cover the bills of public health, western development, rural development and the northeast industrial base after SARS, and to sustain the harmonious development of both economy and society. Where will it come from? As a rule, we don't misappropriate the existing public revenue but adjust an additional amount. Extra fiscal revenue worth hundreds of billions Yuan per year does fill some gaps, but cannot solve all problems. And how the revenue will increase in the future is even unknown. Hence, to issue more treasury bonds is still a solid source of fiscal revenue for us to count on.

Fourth, even if major adjustments are required for macroeconomic policies as macroeconomic situations change, the proactive policy must exit from the stage but has to fade out step by step due to its rigid features, which have formed in the last six years. Just like marching without a stop but to retreat slowly and orderly, the proactive fiscal policy needs a safe, secure and considerate plan for its withdrawal.

Fifth, from what we have done in the past 26 years, we find an important fact that among a number of factors shoring up sustainable rapid growth of China's economy, the most fundamental one that has no counterpart in the traditional system is the system reform. It justifies the basic principle of development economics; namely, system reform is the power and source of economic growth. To sustain this stable and rapid economic growth momentum, we can and should focus on the reform to drive growth and development. Fiscal instruments should also be utilized to support the reform for the goal of sustainable economic growth.

### Second-best choice

From the facts and recognitions mentioned previously, we know that it's impossible to select a best fiscal policy but necessary to select a second-best one. The CEWC, held from the end of 2003 to the beginning of 2004, made a decision that we should continue to implement proactive fiscal policy.[2] Obviously, that decision and the 2004 budgets[3] of fiscal revenue and expenditure proposed at the Second Session of the Tenth NPC were a second-best choice, which is summarized as structural fine-tuning where proactive fiscal policy stays expansionary but it sets about expansion relief and expenditure investment adjustment (Jin Renqing, 2004b).

By "staying expansionary", we mean aiming fiscal policy at demand expansion and economy stimulus. From the 2004 fiscal budget, 319.8 and 110 billion Yuan were allocated, respectively, for the deficit and long-term construction treasury bonds to be issued. Either the fiscal deficit or long-term construction treasury bonds symbolize the expansionary orientation of proactive fiscal policy.

By "relieving expansion", we mean discretionarily and gradually scaling down the fiscal deficit and long-term construction treasury bonds that are arranged for the purpose of proactive policy implementation at the proper time in response to economic changes. For the 319.8 billion Yuan of fiscal deficit in the 2004 fiscal budget, relative to the denominator (GDP in 2004), actual deficit ratio decreases compared with that in 2003. The issue size of long-term construction treasury bonds decreases from 140 billion Yuan in 2003 to 110 billion Yuan in 2004, and will be reduced to 0 step by step in the future. Later the fiscal budget allocates additional 5 billion Yuan for capital construction as a compromise to offset the effect of reduced long-term construction treasury bonds. As a result, the net reduction is actually 25 billion Yuan.

By "adjusting expenditure", we mean extending the revenue from long-term construction treasury bonds for important construction projects to more aspects. The revenue from long-term construction treasury bonds was used directly for important construction projects, but turned to three aspects in the 2004 budget: subsequent investment on important projects under progress, unfinished work on public projects like public health, and major reforms that are planned or urgent to start but delayed due to fund shortage.

## A turning point: dramatic change

As it's not a best choice, the 2004 fiscal policy from the very beginning was under heavy pressure from both the public opinions and the practical activities. For this reason, it's doomed to go through slight but significant changes in its expression and measures over time.

### *Attempts to adjust the orientation*

The attempts made to adjust the orientation of proactive fiscal policy were back earlier in 2002. At that time, the statement was the proactive policy had to "fade out" step by step (Xiang Huaicheng, 2002b).[4] In 2004 when voices against an overheated economy became louder and louder from every corner, the fiscal policy still stuck to its "proactive" (expansionary) track. Even the monetary authority played its best cards against disinflation – raising the legal reserve several times, yet the financial authority held an ambiguous attitude towards public expectations and censures. In fact, whoever knows a little about how government revenue operates understands that it's not the financial authorities who are stubborn to implement proactive fiscal policy for six years, and it's not the fiscal policy that is inappropriate to intervene in the macro-control measures against an overheated economy, but it's the various complicated economic and social factors that bind the financial authorities and limit the room for fiscal policy to operate. How can we cut tight ropes for the fiscal macro control so that the fiscal authority could go back to the "discretionary" track and the fiscal policy could play "upwind" effects? That is an ultimate goal for both the official and the academic circles.

The date, May 27, 2004, is a turning point. On that day the Global Conference on Poverty Reduction held in Shanghai approached to an end. Finance Minister Jin Renqing delivered a speech on an invitation and answered reporters' repeated questions. According to him, our fiscal policy was to shift from proactive to neutral in order to ensure stable and healthy development of China's economy. It was a tremendous change on addressing China's fiscal policy after 1998, arousing echoes from the economic circles and the whole society as well.

After a closer look at what has happened, we find probably it was the sharp economic change ever since April 2004 that offered good timing for proactive fiscal policy to shift its orientation. The expression of so-called "neutral" fiscal policy was finally then settled down. An increase of 43 percent on fixed assets investment in the first quarter and other statistical figures indicated a sudden mounting pressure on overheated investment. Intensive signals of macro control were disclosed at the State Council Executive Meeting held in early April and the meeting of the Political Bureau of CPC Central Committee held in late April. Policy makers didn't quote "overheated", but the Central Bank and other governmental administrations took a series of measures against "overheated investment", either to "inhibit" or "prevent" overheated investment for the goal of a "soft landing". Under such circumstances, if we continued to implement proactive fiscal policy by increasing bond issuance and expanding expenditure mainly on infrastructure construction, we would have imposed "reverse regulation" on overheated investment, or even it would be like pouring oil to the fire. In that case, we will be doubted and asked to quit for sure (Zhang Diken, 2004). Hence, the voice that we should continue to implement proactive fiscal policy is disappearing, while the voice that proactive fiscal policy should "fade out" or "quit" as soon as possible suddenly becomes louder.

### *Meanings of neutral fiscal policy*

As the proactive fiscal policy lasting for six years has to shift its orientation and its title no longer matches its contents after the shift, the next problem is placed on the agenda that the new policy needs a new title to indicate its special shift meaning and distinguish itself from the previous policies. Under such circumstances, neutral fiscal policy comes out.

People are quite familiar with "neutral" just like they are with basic principles of counter-cyclical fiscal policy. The so-called neutral fiscal policy, unlike those tight and expansionary policies, is intended to balance state revenue and expenditure and has neither expansionary nor tight effects on the aggregate social demand. One of the main tasks of the current macro control is that neutral policy should not impose expansionary impact on the economy.

Once the neutral policy is applied and does work as assumed, the necessary measure should be compressing and even eliminating fiscal deficits totaling 319.8 billion Yuan in 2004, but it's easy to recognize and almost no one has confidence in this measure.

The sharp difference between actual national conditions and the fundamental principle regarding the neutral fiscal policy unveils us the following issue: what changes on earth will the actual fiscal arrangements go through after fiscal policy shifts from "proactive" to "neutral"?

It shall be noted that the neutral policy is just an ideally theoretical proposal, and the fiscal revenue and expenditure cannot be completely balanced in reality, as almost no countries have had such a record ever before. "Neutral" is just a goal for fiscal policy to pursue or an ideal level that fiscal policy is committed to reach. In current China, its practical significance lies in that fiscal policy orientation has been adjusted at both layers of public opinions and actual operation: it focused on and went all out for expansion but now it moderately narrows down expansion and gradually inclines to be neutral.

As far as the previously mentioned significance is concerned, China's financial operation has shifted to be neutral long before the neutral policy philosophy is proposed. Taking the 2004 fiscal budget for example (Figure 7.3), the fiscal deficit is still stabilized at its previous scale and fiscal policy is indicated to stay expansionary, but: (1) the actual deficit ratio decreases over the last year as GDP, its denominator, increases; (2) the issuance volume of long-term construction treasury bonds decreases from 140 billion Yuan to 110 billion Yuan, and is expected to reduce to zero in the future; (3) the revenue from long-term construction treasury bonds issued went only to key construction projects but now extends to subsequent investment on important projects under progress, unfinished work on public projects and major reforms that are planned or urgent to start. The 2004 fiscal budget arrangements show a trend of narrowed-down expansion. The neutral policy proposal unveils those previous slight and small adjustments that were done under the table and extends them to macro-control measures on overall government revenue and expenditure and its structure.

### *Setting prudent fiscal policy*

Discussions on neutral fiscal policy have always been carried out from a theoretical perspective. However, when we look back, it's just in the course of discussions that fiscal policy started to shift its orientation. The philosophy of orientation shift of fiscal policy takes shape based on the theoretical discussions.

The CEWC held in early December 2004 finally made the significant decision to shift fiscal policy orientation in 2005 after an overall analysis of current global

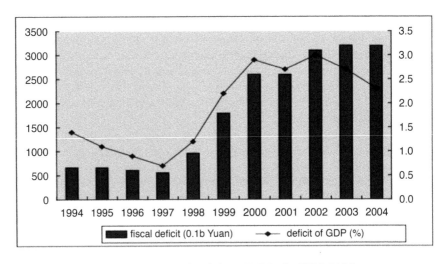

*Figure 7.3* China's Fiscal Deficit and Deficit-to-GDP Ratio (1994–2004)

Sources: Editorial Committee of China's Finance Year Book: *Finance Year Book of China*, China State Finance Magazine, 2002; Ministry of Finance: *Reports on 2004 Central and Local Budget Performance and 2005 Central and Local Budget Draft*, China Securities Journal, March 16, 2005

situations. Later, the CEWC named the policy as prudent fiscal policy. During the process from discussing the neutral policy meanings to naming a prudent fiscal policy, the relation of the two policies becomes obvious so that so-called prudent fiscal policy equals to neutral fiscal policy quoted in economics (Jin Renqing, 2004a). Conceptual achievements made in the discussions on the neutral policy were carried forward under the flag of prudent fiscal policy and put into good practice, especially the progressive concepts that we should appropriately narrow down expansion and gradually approach to neutral. "Moderate tightness" and "double decreases", i.e. the decreases on both fiscal deficit and long-term construction national bonds, are the core and symbols of prudent fiscal policy, according to the CEWC documents.

## Becoming prudent in reform: 2005 fiscal policy orientation

### *A progressive process*

Interestingly, fiscal policy shift didn't start in the 2004 CEWC where fiscal policy was enthusiastically discussed, if the so-called "moderate tightness" and "double decreases" symbolized the fiscal policy orientation shifting from being proactive to being prudent. In fact, the 2004 fiscal budget arrangements implicated the tendency of orientation adjustment of fiscal policy in many aspects, but a series of fiscal measures then were still carried out under the name of prudent fiscal policy. In practice, prudent fiscal policy was to continue and improve those macro-control moves launched over a year ago.

If 2004 saw the prudent policy put in place in the name of being proactive, the 2005 policy was finally called by its right name.

Even when previous slight and small adjustments that were done under the table are put on the stage and macro-control measures are extended to overall government revenue and expenditure and its structure, it doesn't mean we will stop the proactive policy and turn to the prudent overnight. A progressive process might be needed.

Those obstacles and practical issues, repeated over again in this paper, have impeded orientation adjustment of fiscal policy since the beginning of this macro control. They are now believed to be the wake-up call at the government's hand (Gao Peiyong, 2004).

Jin Renqing (2004a) published a paper, "Prudent Fiscal Policy Should be Carried Out to Promote Steady and Rapid Economic Development", shortly after the 2004 CEWC was closed. He concluded the obstacles of prudent policy involving the following aspects: (1) the policy needed to stay consistent so that subsequent investments could be ensured for the treasury bond-invested projects under the process and those unaccomplished ones as they had their own construction cycles; (2) applying the brakes too hard would have adverse impacts on the economy if rapid economic growth, some industries and projects are heavily dependent on treasury bond funds; and (3) many backward aspects needed to be improved in accordance with the "five balanced aspects" (balanced urban and rural development, balanced development among regions, balanced economic and social development, balanced development of man and nature, and balanced domestic development and opening wider to the outside world), and the resources would be concentrated to increase the investment in agriculture, education, public health, social security and ecological environment sectors if the size of the deficit was maintained at a certain level, while exercising macro control would make initiative response to the complicated situations both at home and abroad.

This tough process of fiscal policy shift has already demonstrated the complexity of decision-making in reality. It has to adapt to macroeconomic changes and balance the interests of all stakeholders, build itself upon fiscal revenue and expenditure activities and coordinate with closely-related control measures like the monetary policy and the state plan, conduct counter-cyclical operations targeting one specific sector and weigh up overall situations and goals of different sectors as well, and seek short-term solutions for current realistic contradictions and establish systems for the long run. Limited room is left for prudent fiscal measures as a result.

### *To start from deepening reform*

In order to devise prudent fiscal measures against such a complicated and challenging background, we may have an appropriate and feasible option – to start deepening reform with a series of progressive plans to narrow down expansionary fiscal plans and move closer to prudent fiscal policy, step by step.

The circumstances to be considered are as follows:

First, the fundamental causes are nothing but system defect and structural imbalance when China's current economy is described as either completely or partially overheated. The ultimate solution depends on the implementation of reform actions and the improvement of the market system. At present, people normally believe it's just economic and political cycles that result in over-investment in fixed assets. The shift from a proactive policy to a prudent one must be in alignment with the market-oriented reform process. Prudent measures and plans must be plotted over the chessboard of propelling and deepening reform.

Second, it's not easy to keep the fiscal expenditure scale under control due to the inertial effect of proactive fiscal policy that is implemented for over seven years and the defects of expenditure control systems. The rapid growth of the 2004 revenue boosted all departments' desires to increase their spending and would further raise the overall expenditure levels in 2005 and later. Even if we take progressive prudent measures, we have to narrow down the expansion of fiscal plans after all. Comparatively, the spending on pushing reform measures forward grows in a smaller scale than any others. When the total scale of fiscal expenditure is almost out of control and even soaring, its expansionary effect could be minimized by directing additional spending as much as possible toward the actions  drive reform. The adjustment of spending structure is obviously a good strategy we could exert.

Third, finance always plays the role of trailblazer and paves the way for pushing the overall reform forward in the process of China's marketization reform. At the early stage, the central finance delegated more powers and transferred more interests to lower levels at the cost of central revenue decrease and expenditure increase. It stimulated all parties' enthusiasm for the reform and created favorable conditions for introducing reform measures. At the crucial stage, the 1994 fiscal and tax reform laid a sound foundation for the overall reform, so that it could successfully move towards system innovation. As it was at both early and crucial stages, the fresh task to improve market economic system would depend on the finance for sure. Given the convention and historical experience with how China's finance supported the reform, and given the difficulties and risks of adjusting the current fiscal stock (including the increment), we should drive the reform of overall economic system to success through the imbalanced fiscal revenue and expenditure and the fiscal reform itself.

### *"Sixteen-character" prudence-oriented principle*

To guide the implementation of prudent fiscal policy, the finance ministry has proposed an updated 16-character principle of deficit control, structure adjustment, reform deepening, revenue increase and expenditure decrease (Jin Renqing, 2004b). The 16-character principle should be interpreted under realistic circumstances.

By "deficit control", we mean reducing fiscal deficit and long-term construction treasury bonds to an appropriate level. As discussed previously, we wouldn't do much to cut down either the deficit or long-term construction treasury bonds due to both historical and realistic factors. At the moment, we could barely do anything but push forward reforms to achieve the deficit control step by step.

By "structure adjustment", we mean optimizing the government investment portfolios in accordance with the scientific outlook on development and the construction requirements on public finance. The adjustment will definitely be engaged with both flow and stock of the finance. No matter we deal with problems individually or guarantee consumption demand and suppress investment demand, as well, the structure adjustment should be in line with reform measures and should be achieved by deepening reforms.

By "reform deepening", we mean giving up the economic growth that is shored up or stimulated by fiscal expenditure but focusing on the public finance reform itself and the reform-oriented fiscal arrangements under the flag of "promoting growth and development by reforms", so as to propel the process of overall reform.

By "revenue increase and expenditure decrease", we mean intensifying taxation by collecting taxes payable as much as possible, curbing the trend of overspending growth, and improving the performance of financial funds. This is a regular work for both finance and tax authorities, and also a long-term goal to achieve through reforms.

The 16-character principle logically creates a blueprint for the implementation of prudent fiscal policy and is full of the spirit of reform. Actually, it will be carried out under the keynote of deepening reforms.

## Possible effective room

When deepening reforms is bound up with prudent fiscal policy, and prudent fiscal arrangements are made under the keynote of deepening reforms, the prudent policy will break up various subjective and objective bottlenecks and obtain new achievements.

The bottlenecks include at least the following aspects.

The first is taxation system reform. The necessity to launch another taxation system reform has already been justified. The Third Plenary Session of the Sixteenth CPC Central Committee in 2003 made an overall plan for this new taxation system reform. The main task at present is to take appropriate measures to launch this reform as soon as possible.

The "revenue turbulence" was the primary factor that impeded the new taxation system reform. It means policy makers are worried that tax revenue would decrease due to the reform. Recently the "contrary regulation", another factor, rose. It means that people are worried that overheated fixed asset investment would get even more heated due to reduced tax revenue. How and when to relieve the two worries determines the pace of the introduction of a new taxation reform.

Let's start with the "revenue turbulence". The proposed taxation reform will beyond doubt result in the revenue reduction. Reforms that involve only value-added tax and corporate income tax are estimated to reduce 200 billion Yuan of fiscal revenue. Policy makers are of course very cautious and hesitant when financial funds are predicated to be too short to cover a wide range of investment programs. However, the taxation reform cannot be delayed forever due to the revenue decrease. It would never happen if we insist on the belief that we shouldn't carry out the taxation reform until the financial funds are sufficient.

If we free ourselves from the conventional pattern that taxation reform leads to revenue reduction and look at the whole procedure of fiscal revenue and expenditure, we will discover two correlated facts. One is that China's revenue has grown faster and faster since 1994 and its base has been raised high by the 11-year rapid growth (Figure 7.4). The 2004 revenue is almost 5.9 times that of 1993. The other is that, the government spending grows even much faster than its revenue and its base is expanded with the support of high revenue during the 11 years (Figure 7.5). The 2004 spending is almost 6.5 times that of 1993. It means it is like a "one-way shuttle" that travels from the revenue increase directly to the spending expansion in the last 11 years.

China's tax revenue now reaches its peak after years of rapid growth. We used to believe its high growth resulted from the combination of economic growth, policy adjustment and taxation management enhancement, but things changed in 2004. Policy adjustment, one of the three factors, was replaced by price hikes. Economic growth is still somewhat under control, but the other two factors are absolutely unsustainable. Apart from the cyclic inflation, taxation management enhancement is of concern. The State Administration of Taxation estimates the prevailing taxation system has already raised the actual tax rate by 20 percentage points since its introduction in 1994. Such increase reaches upper limit. Actually, little room is left ahead after the actual tax rate climbed from 50 percent in 1994 to 70 percent now. Therefore, the law of diminishing returns will definitely take effect.

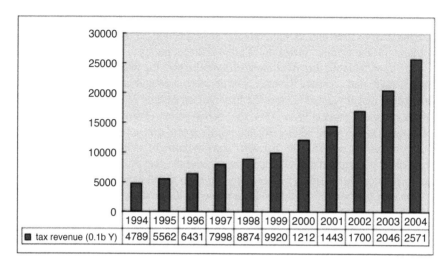

*Figure 7.4* Rapid and Steady Growth of China's Tax Revenue (1994–2004)

Sources: Editorial Committee of China's Finance Year Book: *Finance Year Book of China*, China State Finance Magazine, 2002; Ministry of Finance: *Reports on 2004 Central and Local Budget Performance and 2005 Central and Local Budget Draft*, China Securities Journal, March 16, 2005

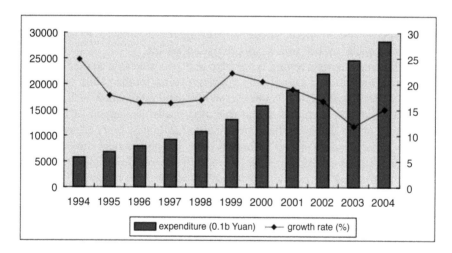

*Figure 7.5* Rapid and Steady Growth of China's Fiscal Expenditure (1994–2004)

Sources: Editorial Committee of China's Finance Year Book: *Finance Year Book of China*, China State Finance Magazine, 2002; Ministry of Finance: *Reports on 2004 Central and Local Budget Performance and 2005 Central and Local Budget Draft*, China Securities Journal, March 16, 2005

Now the tax revenue is on an unprecedented rise. Its high growth would give a rise to an inappropriate expansion of government spending if no good plans were made. A feasible option is to seize the "peak season" of fiscal revenue and contribute the extra-budgetary revenue to the launch of new taxation reform.

Let's move to "contrary regulation". Usually if we need to pay the price of the revenue reduction for the implementation of a new taxation reform, it will take expansionary effect and its implementation, especially at this moment, will contradict with the original intention of prudent fiscal policy.

However, once we turn over the taxation reform at the background of rapid revenue growth and compare the effects of tax decreases and increased spending, we will know that if we had no specific fiscal arrangements against the rapid growth of tax revenue, especially in 2004, the increased tax revenue worth hundreds of billions of Yuan would be directly and totally spent[5] due to the defects of our various systems and would even "activate" the government's vigorous enthusiasm for fixed asset investment that was depressed due to the pressure from public opinion. Its consequent expansionary effect may not be avoided in any case.

The new taxation reform that is implemented at the price of revenue reduction will definitely have expansionary effect, but the basic principle of a balanced budget tells us that apart from tax decrease, expenditure increase also has expansionary effect on the central funds. The latter is comparatively more effective than the former. The potential expansionary consequences of the new taxation reform are not as serious as the inappropriate expansion that is caused by the fact that tax increase turns "directly" to fiscal spending. In this case, the "forward regulation" that moves consistently with prudent fiscal policy is to use the revenue increment to pay for the new taxation reform.

The second is social security system reform, which is a real bottleneck among China's reforms. Others such as reforms of SOEs, rural areas, finance, employment and re-employment systems, cannot be accomplished to a great extent unless social security system reform succeeds. We all agree that neither is its significance understood unclearly, nor is its study process unfeasible.

Social security system reform is bound to cost a considerable amount before its goals are achieved. As a significantly important sector for the public, one system that could benefit all social members cannot be well established without a push from the government, and its sound operation needs the support of the public finance. To obtain that goal, the central finance has to bear more responsibilities and pay more prices than ever before. In short, the government should allocate more funds to this reform. Actually, its process is slowed down and our expectations of its goals are correspondingly lowered as we are short of funds. Even social security fund accounts for subsistence allowances cannot be fully funded.

Whereas the public finance impedes the social security system reform, it does make sense that we take some efforts to push its reform and pay some prices to upgrade its goals during our implementation of prudent fiscal policy. Furthermore, the funds spent on the social security system reform bring less expansionary consequences than that on other issues. It works consistently with the prudent policy under the current circumstances.

The third is rural reform. Balancing urban and rural development always outweighs the other four "balanced aspects" and the new government has always put rural reform first since its leadership.

The development gap was too wide between China's urban and rural regions for a long time. It was narrowed down at the earlier stage of the reform for a while, but not long, and now it keeps widening again. The rural residents accounting for 64 percent of national population have a much lower per capita disposable income than the urban residents and receive a series of unfair treatments. For example, they don't enjoy the same public goods or services as the urban, but have to pay more taxes. We've already anticipated the dangers of these widening gaps long before and know it's not absolutely and objectively impossible to bridge or elimi-nate some of these gaps. Sooner or later, the government should grant farmers with national treatment and then solve problems of agriculture, rural areas and farmers by the means of finance regulation. Of course, the sooner the government starts, the better the rural reform will be.

We're delighted to witness the smooth and fast process of rural reform after 2004. All taxes on agricultural special products were announced to be repealed at once except for tobacco; agricultural taxes were planned to be rescinded in the next three to five years; this year sees a favorable signal that the abolition of agricultural taxes will be accelerated. Twenty-seven provinces, municipalities and autonomous regions have successively canceled their local agricultural taxes up to now. The taxes that have lasted for thousands of years will until late next year step down from the historical stage. The finance funds have been already directed toward farmer-targeted aspects, like the family planning encouragement and assistance system, the new rural cooperative medical system and the medical help system. The public finance is shining on the rural regions step by step. All of these require a significant amount of funding, but these prices are only probable with the support of rapid growth of tax revenue.

Our current task is to catch the rare shuttle of prudent fiscal policy and push the comprehensive and systematic rural reform up to a higher level. If it were done, its double benefits would be known to us as the achievements of both rural reform goals and prudent fiscal policy goals.

(Originally published in *Journal of Renmin University of China*, Vol.5, 2005)

## Notes

1 An example is 2003 long-term construction treasury bonds. We planned to cut down a substantial issuance scale but finally still kept the original scale of 140 billion Yuan due to various factors; as a result, the bond revenue balance at the current year amounted up to 40 billion Yuan, and an extra 1.6 billion Yuan in interest was also paid.
2 The 2003 CEWC stated "we need to maintain consistency and stability in our macroeco-nomic policies, stick to the domestic demand expansion guideline, implement proactive fiscal policy and prudent monetary policy. Funds from the sale of treasury bonds and extra fiscal funds should be directed towards rural areas, the western region, northeast China and other old industrial bases, social security system and poor people's life. More-over, we need to guarantee the key national constructions and support new major reform measures" (People's Daily, December 5, 2003).
3 Premier Wen Jiabao said in the Report on the Work of the Government at the Second Session of the Tenth NPC, "to ensure effective macro-control, we need to maintain con-sistency and stability in our macroeconomic policies while adjusting the intensity and focus of policy implementation at the proper time and to an appropriate degree in

response to developments and changes in the economic situation. By 'at the proper time', we mean seizing the opportune moment for introducing control measures by observing small clues that may indicate what is coming, so as to forestall any possible trouble. By 'to an appropriate degree', we mean that macro-control should neither be too loose nor too tight and that we must not apply the brakes too hard or apply control measures too rigidly" (Wen Jiabao, 2004).

4  The saying that proactive fiscal policy should "fade out" was first publicly delivered by former Financial Minister Xiang Huaicheng on April 15, 2004. He said "proactive fiscal policy should fade out step by step. No government or financial minister could implement proactive fiscal policy for long without causing any troubles" (http://business.sohu.com/51/64/article200736451.shtml).

5  It's an actual case. Under the present systems, up to 406.1 billion Yuan of "extra-budgetary revenue" in 2004 offsets no current fiscal deficit but turns directly into the "extra expenditure".

# References

Cong Ming, Assessment on China's Economic and Fiscal Policies and Financial Risks, *China's Economic and Social Forum, China's Association of Economy and Society*, Vol.2, February 2003

Gao Peiyong, Fiscal Policy Pursues for Breakthroughs, *People's Daily*, December 29, 2003a

Gao Peiyong, Proactive Fiscal Policy: Pursue for Both Philosophical and Initiative Break-through, *Finance & Trade Economics*, Vol. 7, 2003b

General Affairs Department of the Ministry of Finance, *1991–2004 National Debts* (Hard Copy)

Jia Kang, How to Adjust and Cut Down National Debt Scale, *China Taxation News*, May 26, 2004

Jin Renqing, Prudent Fiscal Policy Should Be Carried Out to Promote Steady and Rapid Economic Development, *People's Daily*, March 7, 2004a

Jin Renqing, Reports on 2003 Central and Local Budget Performance and 2004 Central and Local Budget Draft at the Second Session of the Tenth NPC on March 6, 2004, *People's Daily*, March 18, 2004b

Liu Mingkang, Understand the Central Macroeconomic Control Policies Comprehensively, Accurately and Aggressively, *China Securities Journal*, June 25, 2004

Ministry of Finance, Reports on 2004 Central and Local Budget Performance and 2005 Central and Local Budget Draft, *China Securities Journal*, March 16, 2005

Wang Bao'an, Analysis and Shift of China's Current Fiscal Policy, *Finance & Trade Economics*, Vol. 5, 2004

Wei Jianing, Disputes on Macro-economic Control, *FAREN Magazine*, Vol.6, 2004

Wen Jiabao, Report on the Work of the Government at the Second Session of the Tenth NPC on March 5, 2004, *China Securities Journal*, March 17, 2004

Xiang Huaicheng, Proactive Fiscal Policy Is Political Wisdom, *China Times*, August 17, 2002a

Xiang Huaicheng, *Proactive Fiscal Policy Must Fade Out Step by Step*, 2002b, http://business.sohu.com/51/64/article200736451.shtml

# 8 A new round of proactive fiscal policy

## Progress review and tendency forecast

## Preface

Given the law of periodic fluctuations of economic activity and the distinction from proactive fiscal policy implemented from 1998–2004, the policy that started in the fourth quarter of 2008 and now is still in effect is called "a new round of proactive fiscal policy", at least in the academic research field.

Since the day in early November 2008 when it was decided during the State Council Executive Meeting to adjust the orientation of macroeconomic policies, the new round of proactive fiscal policy has so far been implemented in China for 14 months, across two budget years. In fact, the discretionary adjustment of the new round of proactive fiscal policy has been accompanied by frequent profound changes of the Chinese macroeconomy for more than one year. Two events are closely associated and intertwined. It is like a thrilling symphony.

More than a year after the orientation adjustment of macroeconomic policies, during the 2009 Central Economic Work Conference (CEWC) closed not long before, the central government made an important decision to continue to implement proactive fiscal policy and moderately loose monetary policy after completely analyzing the economic situations both at home and abroad. It's estimated, in 2010 and over the long term, this new round of proactive fiscal policy will continue to expand and adapt itself to the updated times, and even play a "more direct, powerful and effective" role in fighting against global finance crisis, sustaining steady and rapid economic development and laying a solid foundation for the launch and implementation of the Eleventh Five-Year Plan.

At the special moment when the previous year is gone and the next year is coming, two associated tasks are challenging us. One is to systematically review the practical progress in the previous year; the other is to forecast the possible tendency in the coming year and even over the longer term. They are the focus of this paper.

The paper is to address three questions. First of all, what features distinguish this new round of proactive fiscal policy from the one implemented from 1998–2004? Second, what specific initiatives were introduced under the flag of proactive fiscal policy, and how did they work in last year? At last, if our macroeconomic policies stay constant and stable, and this new round of proactive fiscal policy holds its orientation unchanged, what more initiatives should we implement in 2010 and over the longer term?

## Practical characteristics of the new round of proactive fiscal policy

In existing textbooks and dictionaries of economics, proactive fiscal policy is not yet clearly defined. Speaking of that, what occurs to us as a reference is the fiscal policy implemented in China from 1998–2004. In the financial crisis in Southeast Asia over a decade ago, we performed expansionary fiscal operations for the purpose of boosting domestic demand under the name of proactive fiscal policy. And during those seven years, through a series of macroeconomic policy arrangements made up of expansionary fiscal operations, we gained 1–2 percent GDP growth per year (Gao Peiyong, 2004), and finally our economy escaped the shadow of deflation and returned to the track of steady and rapid development.

Now we are aware that proactive fiscal policy is just a synonym of expansionary fiscal policy. The first key issue to address is that we should conclude and understand the practical characteristics of this new round of proactive fiscal policy after comparing the similarities and differences between the two policies. In fact, not only at the launch of this new policy, but also during its progress and even today when it has been practiced for over a year and starts to make new practice plans in the next year, this issue should still be addressed.

Compared with the practices from 1998–2004, the characteristics of this new round of proactive fiscal policy can be concluded and understood from the following two aspects.

### The "spiker" of macro control

From 1998–2004, proactive fiscal policy and moderately tight monetary policy constituted our "loose-tight" macroeconomic policy package. When expansionary finance coincides with monetary deflation and when two policy instruments function in opposite directions, it's difficult to say which is primary and which is secondary. Differently, this "dual-loose" package is composed of proactive fiscal policy and moderately loose monetary policy. When fiscal and monetary policies are committed to expand and when two policy instruments function to one direction, one must be primary and the other secondary.

We notice, at present, this global financial crisis already extends to the real economy and evolves into a crisis of global production overcapacity. Moreover, this crisis spreads to the whole world, unlike the last regional crisis which only affected Southeast Asia and excluded the west. In the face of global production overcapacity, we have no way back. The moderately loose monetary policy, which is to lower interest rates and print more money, will be less or considerably less effective in stimulating enterprise investment and resident consumption for sure. After 2009, almost 10 trillion Yuan of additional loans hit a sky-high record but didn't raise the Consumer Price Index (CPI) as expected.[1] It is a good example. When the "dual-loose" macroeconomic policy package works, the expansionary function of monetary policy is somewhat hindered. This special economic phenomenon indicates that in China, encircled by global financial crises, the important responsibility to stimulate domestic demand that used to be shared by two policy instruments is historically more undertaken by the fiscal policy.

Government finance expands its incoming and outgoing activities by "increasing expenditure + decreasing taxes". Unlike the transmission mechanism of the monetary policy, fiscal expenditure increase or tax revenue decrease is always under the direct control of governments. In addition, financial gains and losses themselves can be given up for the sake of macroeconomic benefits if necessary. Such distinctive functions of fiscal policy are put into full use in this rare global financial crisis.

Looking into the practices of countermeasures against the global financial crisis so far, we may find not only the Chinese government but other global governments put forward a series of "economic revitalization" or "economic stimulus" measures to fight against their financial crises. These measures cover a large variety of economic areas, but fall mainly within the scope of fiscal policy. That is to say, in the last year, China's battle to stabilize growth pushed this new round of proactive fiscal policy to the forefront of macro control and consolidated its position of "spiker".

In summary, this is the first outstanding feature of this new round of proactive fiscal policy that it should undertake the job of "spiker" in the macro-control system against the global financial crisis.

### Two-pronged expansion

As discussed previously, fiscal policy is always executed through the carriers of public revenue and spending. To be specific, the expansionary fiscal policy is usually implemented throughout the work of "collecting less" (i.e. "less tax") on one side and "spending more" (i.e. "more spending") on the other side. In short, "more spending + less tax" is almost the entire contents of expansionary fiscal policy.[2]

During the period from 1998–2004, all social sectors never stopped their cries for tax cuts; nevertheless, the proactive fiscal policy at that time only focused on "more spending", which was financed by the issuance of long-term construction treasury bonds. If the previous policy had attached its importance only to more public expenditure but did little or even nothing on public revenue, especially tax cuts, this new policy would value both expenditure and revenue.

The CEWC convened in early December 2008, defining the contents of this new fiscal policy as "increasing substantial public spending and implementing structural tax cut". Since then, it has started a series of expansionary fiscal moves, which include conventional measures to expand fiscal spending and new ones for structural tax cuts. As far as how to expand fiscal spending is concerned, we can increase government-funded projects, increase incomes for low and medium earners, and sell household electric appliances and vehicles at discount in villages as well. As far as the structural tax cut is concerned, tax categories with larger shares like Value-Added Tax (VAT) and the merger of two Corporate Income Taxes (CITs) are involved, as are those with smaller shares like Personal Income Tax (PIT), second-handed housing transaction taxes, and stamp taxes on stock trading. Briefly, this new round of proactive fiscal policy implemented now takes advantage of almost all expansionary measures, including "more spending" and "less tax".

In summary, this is the second outstanding feature of this new round of proactive fiscal policy, i.e. it should emphasize and implement two-pronged measures for fiscal expansion.

## Practices in the previous year: a rough list

It might be necessary to review what has been done under the expansionary fiscal policy over the past year or so. It involves "more spending" and "less tax" done in two budget years (Ministry of Finance, 2009).

### *Increase public spending*

Let's start with "more spending". In early November 2008 when the State Council Executive Meeting decided to adjust orientation of macroeconomic policies, there was less than two months in that budget year for the government to take expansionary fiscal moves. In such a short period of time, the government unveiled two emergent measures to boost "more spending". One was to add a new arrangement that the central government set aside 104 billion Yuan beyond the original 2008 budget to invest in affordable housing projects. The other was to put the arrangement ahead of schedule that 20 billion Yuan allocated for post-earthquake reconstruction was moved from the 2009 budget to the 2008 budget. The two arrangements combined increased public spending by 124 billion Yuan.

In 2009, five efforts were intensified to introduce various initiatives, one by one, to boost spending:

First, spend more on government-funded projects. Except for the additional 124 billion Yuan of investment on affordable housing projects and post-earthquake reconstruction at the end of 2008, the central government added 487.5 billion Yuan for public investment. If public spending planned as usual is included, the central government invested a total of 908 billion Yuan in 2009. That includes 208 billion Yuan for agricultural infrastructure and rural livelihood projects; 49.3 billion Yuan for affordable housing projects; 71.3 billion Yuan for education, health and social undertakings; 130 billion Yuan for post-earthquake reconstruction; 68 billion Yuan for energy saving and ecological construction; 45.2 billion Yuan for self-dependent innovation, technological upgrading and service business development; and 231.7 billion Yuan for railways, roads, airports, harbors and other infrastructure.

Second, allocate more subsidies for farmers. An additional 20.04 billion Yuan was set aside, an increase of 19.4 percent over the previous year. That included direct subsidies for grain producers, general subsidies for agricultural supplies, subsides for superior crop varieties and purchase subsidies for farm machinery. In addition, 20 billion Yuan and 5 billion Yuan of subsidies were respectively allocated for selling household electrical appliances and vehicles to rural areas.

The central finance contributed a total of 148.08 billion Yuan in subsidies of all varieties to farmers.

Third, allocate more subsidies for low and medium earners in cities. An additional 220.833 billion Yuan was spent for this purpose through raising subsistence allowances for needy rural and urban residents, giving one-time subsidies to needy rural and urban households with difficulties before the Spring Festival, increasing pensions for enterprise retirees, raising benefits and subsistence allowances for those who are entitled to special care by the government, and directly giving one-time living subsidies to people with difficulties.

Fourth, spend more on guarantee and improvement work on people's livelihood. For example, the central finance appropriated 716.14 billion Yuan in agriculture, rural areas and farmers (120.59 billion Yuan – or 20.2 percent – more than last year); 728.463 billion Yuan in education, healthcare, social security, employment, affordable housing, culture and livelihood projects directly associated with people's lives, (165.334 billion Yuan – or 29.4 percent – more than last year).

Fifth, spend more on science and technological innovation and energy-saving projects. For example, the central finance allocated 146.103 billion Yuan in science and technology programs (29.774 billion Yuan – or 25.6 percent – more than last year); 20 billion Yuan of interest subsidies for enterprises to accelerate their technological transformation and upgrading; 49.5 billion Yuan in supporting energy saving and cleaning out outdated capacity; and 9.6 billion Yuan in helping the development of small and medium-sized enterprises.

### *Implement structural tax cut*

Now let's move to "less tax". It was January 1, 2008 when the tax cut actions were started. The symbol was the implementation of new CIT, after the merger of two tax systems. The earliest tax cut was just a part of the new taxation reform and implemented under the name of taxation reform. After that, as the US subprime mortgage crisis spread into a global finance crisis, the concept of structural tax cut was born and became an important work of this new round of proactive fiscal policy. Next, actions were taken.

Under such circumstances, a series of moves were taken one after another, cutting in total up to 280 billion Yuan of taxes in 2008. These moves were to raise the salary threshold for personal income tax, to suspend personal income taxes on interest earnings from savings and security account balances, to reduce housing transaction taxes, to raise export rebate rates of some products, to cancel and reduce export duties on some products, to lower stamp tax rates on security transactions and impose unilateral taxes, to adjust automobile consumption tax policies, to allow enterprises with difficulties to provisionally delay their social security contributions, and to lower the rates of four social security charges.

Based on that, 2009 had a structural tax cut on a larger scale. On the one hand, new tax relief measures were introduced, like implementing a consumption type of VAT all around and reforming taxes and charges on refined oil products, abolishing and terminating 100 administrative charges; on the other hand, original tax relief policies were continued, like maintaining the salary threshold for personal income tax raised in 2008, raising export rebate rates of some products, canceling and reducing export duties on some products, lowering stamp tax rates on security transactions and imposing unilateral taxes, suspending personal income taxes on interest earnings from savings and security account balance, and reducing housing transaction taxes. In short, nine tax and charge programs were involved, relieving 550 billion Yuan of tax burdens on enterprises and residents.

Comparing such a big tax cut with our fiscal revenue, expenditure and 2009 budget, we find that 550 billion Yuan accounts for 8.3 percent of national fiscal revenue (6.623 trillion Yuan, with 50.5 billion Yuan from the Central Budget Stabilization Fund excluded), and 7.2 percent of national expenditure (7.6235 trillion Yuan). It is quite a big number in any case.

The previously mentioned rough list unveils the fact that this new round of proactive fiscal policy is no longer theoretical but workable through a series of concrete actions.

Such expansionary fiscal measures come out and are put into practice one after another, playing a decisive role in turning our economy upward now. If the rise of the Chinese economy and the effective stop of economic growth decline were attributable to our macroeconomic policies (Zhu Zhixin et al., 2009), we would say the main stimulus of those policies actually comes from this new round of proactive fiscal policy.

## Basic judgment: to change or not to change

We review our history; then we plan our future. We look back at how this new round of proactive fiscal policy distinguished itself and worked over the previous year; then we answer the question of how will it go on in 2010 and even in the long run.

According to discussions of the CEWC, conclusions are quite obvious, as follows:

First, given that the global economy is still unstable and the global financial crisis is still happening at present, and given that Chinese economy has not yet shown a steady uptrend and still needs stimulus of macroeconomic policies, it's of vital importance for us to continue to implement proactive fiscal policy and keep the policy unshifted. In brief, this new policy implemented for over a year should and has to stay expansionary for a longer time.

Second, macroeconomic policies have to adapt to the economic changes as they are always on guard against headwind. Despite their unchanged orientation, it doesn't mean their results in the last year will be copied in 2010. Actually, this new fiscal policy kept changing its contents during the previous year. Likewise, it has to adjust its intensity, pace and emphasis in line with new situations and changes in 2010 – even throughout the period – so that its orientation stays unchanged.

It is an important feature of the new round of proactive fiscal policy in 2010 and even in the long run to make new arrangements and put them into practice under the unchanged orientation.

We may outline the prospect of the new round of proactive fiscal policy in 2010.

The first constant should be the expansionary momentum of fiscal policy. As long as the economy continues to expand when macroeconomy has no fundamental changes yet, the work on more spending and less tax should be equally valued and developed. In other words, the two-pronged fiscal expansion should stay unchanged. Furthermore, since we need constant simulative effects of macroeconomic policies, this new round of proactive fiscal policy still has to play the vital role in the macro control system when macroeconomic policy package has no essential changes. Its role of "spiker" should not be changed.

The first variable should be the core of the policy. By far, the main measures to achieve more spending and less tax have always been anchored in directly increasing public investment and indirectly fueling civil investment. It is quite necessary; however, when our current macro control shifts from stabilizing economic growth to transforming economic stimulus, our economy is able to have a stable recovery only after the consumption demand is finally boosted and driven back to its normal track. As a result, no matter if discussing to increase spending or cut taxes, a pressing issue right now is to move the center of the new round of proactive fiscal policy from investment to consumption demand stimulus in an appropriate time. Additionally, as the global economic downturn ends, the most difficult time is already past, but inflation is increasingly expected to rise, and the new expansionary policy should loosen its intensity and slow its pace in an appropriate time during the changes.

No matter if the constant or the variable factor is concerned, the primary fact that we cannot avoid is the short-term fiscal constraint, which is what we have to pay for implementing a new policy. In the anti-crisis years, an economic downturn or even an economic growth drop would cut down financial revenue and increase financial expenses; moreover, the expansion-oriented financial policy plans are carried out to increase spending and cut taxes and will definitely result in unbalanced financial payment.

To face up to such facts, we need to re-emphasize the overall but pass over local gains and losses. Our history has demonstrated that we would rather suffer from unbalanced financial payment in order to get stable economic and social development in return if necessary. We should always abide by such a rule when we select an appropriate fiscal policy. Now this is not an exceptional case. When the overall economic and social development is valued, it's quite worthy of the price of more short-term financial difficulties if an economic recovery and then a steady and rapid growth would be gained anyhow in return soon. However, if we were content with the unstable economic upturn and faltered in our determination to continue a new round of proactive fiscal policy due to worries about more financial difficulties, or if we were hesitant to deepen and improve the reform of the new round of proactive fiscal policy, the fiscal revenue drop and expense rise caused by a sluggish economy would be impossible to turn around, let alone considering that economic growth would be weaker and the economic slump would be worse. In other words, our short-term difficulties are exchanged for both rapid stable economic growth and development mode transformation; with a solid economy, our fiscal budget will be no longer tight.

## Suggestions: more spending in 2010

So here it is: we have to answer the question now of how we should carry out the new round of proactive fiscal policy in 2010 and later. Still, we need to explain it from two aspects: more spending and less tax.

In terms of more spending, the first thing that occurs to us is the conventional measure for fiscal expansion: to increase expenditure on government-funded projects. The second thing that occurs to us is the so-called "4 trillion investment plan", one of the measures carried out against this crisis. Most people assume that 4 trillion Yuan is about to be spent on additional government-financed projects. However, based on the last year's practical progress, we find that some facts probably should be clarified.

The first is not all 4 trillion Yuan goes to government investment projects. Our government cannot afford investment spending of 4 trillion Yuan due to its limited disposable financial resources at present (it's said before that national revenue and expenditure was merely 6.623 trillion Yuan and 7.6235 trillion Yuan, respectively, in 2009 when expansionary fiscal policy was implemented). Actually, to take actions against this crisis, our central government can allocate only 1.18 trillion Yuan from its fiscal budget to target at public investment projects. The 4 trillion Yuan is just an estimated sum of series of investment projects probably inferred from the 1.18 trillion Yuan of government investment spending. It's just a figure estimated according to the theory of investment pull effect.

The second is that the 1.18 trillion Yuan is not what our central government spends on investment within one year. Our central finance cannot afford investment spending of 1.18 trillion Yuan within one year due to its own limited disposable resources at present (for example, the central finance spent in total 1.4976 trillion Yuan in 2009). In fact, the 1.18 trillion Yuan of public investment spending is appropriated in three years against the crisis. The plan goes to 104 billion Yuan for 2008, 487.5 billion Yuan for 2009, and 588.5 billion Yuan for 2010.

The third is that even public investment spending for a specific year – for example, 487.5 billion Yuan for 2009 – cannot go to instant projects. According to a universal operational rule, the fund for a specific government-financed project has to go through three phases from its allocation to its final usage. In each phase it's the fund in transit, in full payment and in an ongoing project. The fund in transit refers to the government investment budget in process of internal transference of our fiscal system; the fund in full payment refers to that already transferred to the construction companies from our fiscal system; the fund in an ongoing project refers to that spent on specific project by the construction companies. It's obvious that only when it moves to the third phase when it's already spent on ongoing projects that the government investment fund itself and its potentially induced investment would finally exert their effects. The government investment itself, from its fund in transit, in full payment and then in ongoing projects, is likely to take a long time, if measured by the law of public investment.

With so many words, we are simply trying to make a statement on the government fund for public investment as follows. Regarding the measures to increase

2010 fiscal expenditure, we should neither overstate nor fetishize the public investment effect, and above all, we should pay greater attention to the latent outcomes caused by its time-lag factor and do our best to avoid them. Today when macroeconomic conditions change at every moment, the possible time-lag effect of government investment budgeting would spoil our opportunity to boost our economy, and provoke "reverse regulation" where the expansionary effect that should have been occurred in economic downturn is actually postponed until economic upturn. The effect of "reverse regulation" may fuel expectations for inflation as a result. Such conjectures have been confirmed by our practices last year in increasing expenditure on public investment.

On this account, we should shift our government's focus to boost expenditure from the public investment sector to the public consumption sector in 2010. Apart from allocating the necessary funds to ensure those ongoing government-financed projects are completed, our government should extend its additional investment targets towards the support for people's livelihood and social undertakings, and focus on stimulating final consumption demand.

If studied further, we would find income groups vary substantially in their consumption demands, and therefore, it's necessary and also possible to develop different strategies for different income groups to boost their spending.

For low-income earners, it's the relatively low incomes that restrain their demands for consumption. We can "give them money directly" by increasing their disposable income through our fiscal plans for more spending. We expect a big boost to their consumption demands from their increased disposable incomes. For example, in order to increase the purchasing power of those in the low-income brackets, we should ensure the new round of proactive fiscal policy functions effectively in regulating the pattern of national income distribution, and extend the fiscal subsidies to a wider coverage so as to substantially increase the incomes of urban and rural residents who live on subsistence allowances. That would raise the share of personal income in the distribution of national income, and the share of work remuneration in primary distribution, and narrow down the income distribution gap. Besides, we should optimize the structure of government investment spending and focus particularly on the projects affecting the peoples' livelihoods, infrastructure and energy efficiency, and environmental projects in order to pull and lead consumption demand and then boost economic growth.

For middle- and high-income earners, it's the inadequate social security system that inhibits their demands for consumption. We can "pay bills for them" by establishing an effective social security system covering healthcare, pension and education through our fiscal plans for more spending. And we should keep improving the social security system and relieving their worries in order to stimulate their spending. For example, we should further optimize the structure of fiscal expenditure and accelerate social constructions for improving people's livelihood. That would stabilize and raise consumer expectations, increase immediate consumption and stimulate consumption demands. And we should further adjust the structure of fiscal expenditure, strictly control regular spending, and increase our spending – particularly on agriculture, rural areas and farmers, education, employment, housing, healthcare, social security and other peoples' livelihood sectors. Finally, we should actively explore effective financial security modes, establish and improve long-term efficient mechanisms to ensure and better serve the people's livelihoods according to the development rule of social course and the characteristics of public services.

## Suggestions: less tax in 2010

Talking about "tax cut", even the "structural tax cut" strictly defined at present, we need to clarify two issues at first if its effect is measured against enlarging consumption demand, particularly final consumption demand. Both issues are how many tax categories and how much tax our government intends to cut. The former comes down to the tax items, and the latter, the tax revenue scale. They are totally different.

Here, we can take our 2008 tax revenue scale for example. Except for only one item, the fixed asset investment regulation tax which is exempted temporarily, there are 18 effective tax categories in our current taxation system. A statistical report issued by the State Administration of Taxation (SAT) in 2008 says our national tax revenue was 5.7862 trillion Yuan and VAT took a 42.7 percent share, ranking No. 1; CIT 21.2 percent, business tax 13.2 percent; PIT 6.4 percent; consumption tax 5.7 percent; and the rest, in total, no more than 10.8 percent.

It's not hard to notice, no matter if examining 2010 or later, that if we want to boost consumption demand, especially final consumption demand, we should focus on how much tax rather than how many tax categories our government has cut. Therefore, when addressing China's tax reduction issue and designing solutions, we should highlight the tax categories with bigger shares, namely VAT, CIT, business tax, PIT and consumption tax. The revenue from these taxes amounts to nearly 90 percent of our national tax revenue.

These major taxes vary sharply from each other, so they need different tax reduction plans. Business tax, the third in the share rank, is a main category of local governments and the root of our current tax-sharing system whereby the tax revenue is divided by central and local governments. It's better not to make a big change until we have resolved to carry out a radical reform of our current tax-sharing system. Consumption tax, the fifth in the share rank, is not a separate tax but a supplementary tax. It functions to regulate consumption and narrow down the wealth gap. General speaking, it's better to increase rather than to decrease consumption taxes if we want to intensify the taxation regulation as our current system is relatively too weak. What we can do something about, finally, are only VAT, CIT and PIT.

The CIT reform is almost successful and has already made some incredible achievements in the defense against the global financial crisis; we will continue to improve supporting policies for CIT laws in 2010. Let's mainly discuss VAT and PIT.

VAT is the biggest tax in China. To obtain a substantial cut of taxes, of course, we should and have to concentrate on VAT. Since January 1, 2009, it has been implemented nationwide and made significant effect on enterprises to transform the production-type VAT to a consumption type. After the VAT reform, the payments on new fixed assets purchased by enterprises can be deducted from the VAT base, and thus are VAT exempt. This move encourages additional investment on fixed assets and also implies this as the biggest bill of tax cut that our government can afford. About 120 billion Yuan of taxes is estimated to be reduced per year by this move.

However, we should notice, the VAT reform, different from the reduction measures on other tax categories, is a policy introduced by our government to relieve the tax burden of enterprises and boost their investment, after all. Apart from a small number of enterprises who are directly taxed at a lower rate, whether most enterprises can enjoy the expected benefits or how many benefits they can actually enjoy from this policy, it's up to their response to the VAT reform. Enterprises would only enjoy an offset of VATs payable if they really embark on technology upgrades and expand equipment investment. And the reduced taxes from the VAT reform would be cashable benefits that go into the pockets of enterprises. The potential benefits are like a bird released by our government and flying in the forest. It cannot be caught by our enterprises unless they do adjust their investment behaviors, and their adjustments are as good as expected.

The tricky thing is that enterprises have inadequate desires or motives for investment due to global overcapacity; therefore, we have to underestimate the ultimate reduction effect of the VAT reform and keep some contingencies at hand. If the VAT reform did not achieve a tax cut in 2009 as expected, and more powerful expansionary measures were needed for taxation with the changes of economy, we would give up more benefits to enterprises in the 2010 VAT reform by dividing the spending on houses and buildings into the deduction scope and permitting the offset of input VAT paid on fixed asset investment in full amount. In 2010, a consumption-based VAT would be then collected in an absolute sense.

Now let's move to PIT. In our actual pattern of tax revenue, the PIT share is not too big as a modern tax with both revenue collection and regulation functions, but people are more sensitive to this tax than any other taxes, especially those turnover taxes concealed in commodity prices and collected indirectly. The fact is, of course, related to the weak tax awareness and misunderstanding of our taxpayers. In the global financial crisis, our government has raised the income tax personal allowance threshold and then temporarily exempted the tax on interest earnings from individual deposits, resulting in a tax relief of 46 billion Yuan per year, but people still expect more from a further alleviation of the PIT burden. It's hence very necessary to answer to people's long-cherished aspiration in the long run.

Whereas a small step of the PIT fine-tuning, i.e. the threshold raise, has almost come to its end; whereas the PIT fine-tuning has not effectively alleviated the burdens of low and middle-income earners; and whereas this new tax system reform has already determined the direction that both comprehensive and classified income tax systems should be combined together and that the tax reduction intention should echo with tax reform goals, an important fact that we can confirm is both the income tax burden alleviation and the tax reform should undergo major surgery. We should take substantial measures as soon as possible to widen the coverage and accelerate laying the foundation of comprehensive tax. Regarding it as a trigger, we will carry out "personal" deductions for income taxes and stipulate regulations governing personal deductions, thereby regulating the income distribution gap by making high earners pay more taxes than low earners.

As a matter of fact, this move is going to take hold, anyway, according to the development law of the personal income tax system. This is an inevitable trend. In 2010, it will and should be our alternative plan to create favorable conditions and take this move as soon as possible.

(Originally published in *Finance & Trade*
*Economics*, Vol. 1, 2010)

## Notes

1 As of the end of October 2009, our CPI was still negative; it didn't turn to be positive, at 0.6 percent, until the end of November.
2 Theoretically both fiscal deficit and national debts are financing options. They can not only support the expanded public spending but also offset tax cuts. Thus, strictly speaking, only higher expenditure and lower taxes are the first content of expansionary fiscal policy.

## References

Editorial Committee of China's Tax Year Book, *2008 China Taxation Yearbook*, China Taxation Publishing House, 2009

Gao Peiyong, From Proactive to Neutral: A Tough Choice for Fiscal Policy, *Recent Discussions on Orientation of Fiscal Policy*, Vol.8, 2004

Ministry of Finance, Report on 2008 Central and Local Budget Implementation and 2009 Central and Local Budget Draft at the Second Session of the Eleventh NPC on March 5, 2009, *Xinhua News Agency*, March 15, 2009

Zhu Zhixin et al., Zhu Introduces Our Current Macroeconomic Situations at a State Council Information Office Press Conference, August 7, 2009, http://finance.people.com.cn/GB/9812309.html

# 9 Current economic situation and 2012 fiscal policy

## Preface

The once-a-year Central Economic Work Conference (CEWC) has always been confronted with two issues. One is to evaluate China's current economic situation, and the other is to design economic policies for the next year. The CEWC, held at the end of 2011 completed those routine matters. It made an inclusive evaluation of the world's economic situation, then outlined plans for continuing to implement proactive fiscal policy and prudent monetary policy.

The global financial crisis has lasted for four years so far since 2008 when the US investment bank Lehman Brothers declared bankruptcy. Throughout the four years, our macroeconomic policy, determined at each CEWC, kept amending its principles against the evolving global financial crisis. Let's review the four principles, as follows:

- The 2008 CEWC decided to maintain steady rapid economic growth by implementing a proactive fiscal policy and a moderately loose monetary policy.
- The 2009 CEWC decided to maintain the macroeconomic policies constant and steady by continuing the proactive fiscal policy and moderately loose monetary policy.
- The 2010 CEWC decided to give top priority to speeding up the change in the mode of economic development by implementing a proactive fiscal policy and a prudent monetary policy.
- The 2011 CEWC decided to seek progress while keeping performance stable by continuing the proactive fiscal policy and prudent monetary policy.

Shown by the historical track record of the last four years, China's macroeconomic policies have been implemented as a "proactive and moderately loose" policy package, then the similar "proactive and moderately loose" policy package, then a "proactive and prudent" policy package and then the similar "proactive and prudent" policy package.

A wide margin exists between the name and reality of our government's macroeconomic policies, after all. To be specific, the policy described as "proactive" does not necessarily intend to take expansionary but indeed, probably "prudent" measures. Similarly, the policy described as "prudent" does not necessarily intend to take neutral actions but in fact likely expansionary or tight measures. More specifically, even the macroeconomic policies with identical or matching names often contain totally different intentions. "To continue to implement the policies in the next year" does not equal to copy all policy arrangements in that year. This expression might imply evident adjustments or changes in both economic aggregate and structure.

In short, we should not and cannot interpret our macroeconomic policies by their names. The purpose of this paper is to look into the actual arrangements over the names of macro policies, recognize and understand the world's current economic situation and the CEWC spirit, and then draw out the road map for 2012 proactive fiscal policy.

## Current economic situation: four basic judgments

About the current global economic situation, people have arrived at a consensus that this ongoing upheaval in American and European economies is a huge shock to the global economy that is yet still in slow recovery. This shock will hardly be eliminated in short term, and will probably last for long (Li Yang, 2011). How will the Chinese economy go in the future under such circumstances? We need to, no doubt, answer this question.

First of all, we should notice the profound change and development of economic globalization. The deteriorating and complicated global economic conditions will definitely encumber China's economy which is already drawn into the stream of globalization. More importantly, the globalization process still moves on and its impact is extending; thus, our economy is likely to see a drop in its growth rate, given the cooling foreign demand and insufficient domestic demand, and given that the efforts to transfer the mode of economic development are ineffective in a short time. In other words, China's economy cannot protect itself from the consequences of a global crisis. Its future is quite unpredictable.

Second, the up-to-now track of this global financial crisis reveals that it was definitely the hardest times for the worldwide economies including China from the end of 2008 to the beginning of 2009. After a review of the global economic turbulence, compared with the economy in that darkest period, we could confirm the American and European economies are neither absolutely incurable nor have no way out in spite of their difficulties getting rid of constant upheaval. The external uncertainties would cause a persistent adverse impact on China's economy – but at a macroeconomic level, not more adverse than that between the end of 2008 and the beginning of 2009.

In addition, other emerging economies suffer from the excess liquidity which resulted from a large number of unconventional incentives, but a different story is told in China where the current price hike is driven by an inflationary factor and a cost rise as well. Both inflation pull and cost push on price increase can hardly be relieved in a short time, and they will keep our Consumer Price Index (CPI) at a high level in the long run. More seriously, in today's China, if the price hike coincides with various social conflicts represented by the income distribution inequity, it would, according to Premier Wen Jiabao (2011), threaten social stability and people's faith in our power. In summary, the price level relatively outweighs the economic growth for well-maintained social stability, thus the price hike is still our primary conflict.

Finally, the negative effects of extensive expansion on our economic structure have been increasingly obvious after several anti-crisis operations including government spending increases and public investment expansion. Now the task of economic structure adjustment seems more urgent than what it was before the crisis. Given that this global financial crisis is attributed to the structural imbalance of the global economy; given that China becoming trapped in this crisis is attributed to the same soft spot, a structural imbalance of our economy; and given that the structural imbalance cannot be effectively solved in a short time for both global and Chinese economies, we are in a tough dilemma whether to seek steady economic growth or adjust economic structure, under the pressure of the external prolonged slump and the internal conventional structure becoming unsustainable.

## Dance between "proactive" and "prudent": a play stage for fiscal policy

The previous analysis indicates that 2012 macroeconomic policy literally states to "continue to implement" both proactive fiscal policy and prudent monetary policy; nevertheless, compared with what was done in 2011, its actual arrangements should and have to make considerable adjustments against the substantial changes of global economic situation. Such considerable adjustments include at least the following:

First, the macro control at present gives top priority to pre-tuning and fine-tuning, and its expansionary activities could be carried out in no hurry. It is not necessary to introduce such massive over-expansionary measures into the market as were undertaken at the end of 2008 and the beginning of 2009. We ought not to or should not overreact.

Second, today's changes of the world's economic situation are not enough to alter the order of objectives of our macroeconomic policy started in 2011. In other words, basing ourselves on China's reality, we should still give first priority to stabilizing general price levels after weighing it against economic growth.

Third, even if our economy shows signs of downturn, even if one of the objectives of our macroeconomic policy is to intensify policy stimulus, the expansionary measures should be embodied in seeking a balance between steady growth and structural adjustment. In short, we should never repeat the mistake of sacrificing structural adjustment goals for steady economic growth.

When the specific arrangements of a proactive fiscal policy are concerned, we may check out their outcomes against the fiscal deficit from the perspective of economic aggregate and against the fiscal revenue and expenditure from the perspective of economic structure.

If from the perspective of economic aggregate, we could start with the increased and decreased amounts of our budgetary deficit, because the strength of fiscal expansion directly determines the scale and marginal effect of our budgetary deficit. Budgetary deficit greater than that in the previous year means this year's fiscal policy inclines to be described as expansionary; the same as that of last year, means this year's policy is neutral; and if less than that in last year, means this year's policy is tight.

If working from the perspective of economic structure, we could start with the contrast between spending increase and tax reduction. Under a given scale of budgetary deficit, we are left with only two alternatives: to increase spending, or to reduce taxes. Generally speaking, given the multiplicative difference between spending and tax revenue, spending increase takes more efficient and direct effect on expansion, while tax reduction takes a more soft and indirect effect on expansion.

Now, basing ourselves on the world's current economic situation and the previously mentioned principles of our macroeconomic policy, we could outline a road map for 2012 proactive fiscal policy arrangements from clues of both economic aggregate and structure.

In the matter of economic aggregate, if the deficits offset by treasury bonds and by the Central Budget Stabilization Fund are consolidated, the 2012 budgetary deficit would be equal to or experience a small rise over the 2011 deficit. This is an implication that the strength of fiscal expansion will be constrained. Consequently, the previous full or massive expansion won't be repeated. According to 2011 national fiscal budget statistics (Ministry of Finance, 2011), the deficits offset in that year by treasury bonds and by the Central Budget Stabilization Fund amounted, respectively, up to 900 billion Yuan and 150 billion Yuan, totaling 1.05 trillion Yuan. The 2012 budgetary deficit should be slightly above 1.05 trillion Yuan.

If we proceed with fiscal expansion from economic structure, we should focus on "tax reduction" rather than "spending increase" as the major carrier. The interchange of positions of both expansionary carriers signifies a relative slowdown of fiscal expansion, and more importantly, the compatibility or integration of both implementing fiscal expansion and promoting structural adjustment. In summary, as a major carrier to implement fiscal expansion, we choose "tax reduction" whereby private disposable income is increased, rather than "spending increase" where direct governmental investment is increased. It helps to achieve the goal of "steady growth" and the efficiency of "structural adjustment". In that case, taxes to be reduced in 2012 should be at least 600 billion Yuan, if the total budgetary deficit is estimated to be little more than 1.05 trillion Yuan.

By the way, the 2011 national fiscal revenue figures published recently imply an "excessive revenue" amount up to 1.402 trillion Yuan, when it was calculated on the basis of 10.374 trillion Yuan of national fiscal revenue. The excessive amount takes 13.5 percent and 67.9 percent shares, respectively, of the current year's total national fiscal revenue and increased national revenue. No doubt, it will further push up the controversial overall tax burden level in current China; thus, we will be under greater pressure imposed from the public who are asking for tax reduction. Even though we have taken a series of factors affecting fiscal expansion implementation into consideration, it's not only necessary but also probably for us to cut a certain amount of taxes with such fiscal revenue. In short, we have the necessity and also the capability to cut a large amount of taxes in 2012.

From the latent effects of both economic aggregate and structure, we can identify the overall development of proactive fiscal policy to be implemented in 2012. It is dancing between "proactive" and "prudent" (or "expansionary" and "neutral"). On the one hand, given the uncertainty of the global economic situation – especially the downturn of our economic growth – we are required to take a proactive response. Hence, we should reserve certain room for fiscal expansion. On the other hand, given the pressure of inflation and the necessity of economic structural adjustment, we are required to maintain a neutral effect of the "proactive and prudent" macroeconomic policy package. Hence, we should keep the strength of the fiscal expansion under appropriate control. To summarize, there is a belt where "proactive" or "expansionary" policy is at one end while "prudent" or "neutral" policy is at the other end. This belt becomes the stage for proactive 2012 fiscal policy.

## Structural tax reduction meets the taxation reform head-on

Structural tax reduction is up to now the formal wording regarding tax reduction from the government. As a cliché lasting for at least a dozen years (Jin Renqing, 2002), this is not the first time that structural tax reduction has been tried to spur fiscal expansion. It was incorporated into anti-crisis operations earlier in the later period of the 1990s as an important element of proactive fiscal policy. Again it has spread like wildfire due to the global financial crisis starting from 2008 and played an important role in the anti-crisis activities. However, during the two periods mentioned before, structural tax reduction is not the center of proactive fiscal policy. It plays a supplementary role in the proactive fiscal policy, which concentrates on governmental spending increase and public investment expansion.

Now when the cliché repeats and the previous supporting role turns into a leading role, structural tax reduction should be done more like art. We shall neither cut indiscriminate taxes nor impose the same reduction in any taxes. Obviously, structural tax reduction is unlike general tax reduction. It stands out for its double standards. On the one hand, it aims to alleviate the actual tax burdens for enterprises and individuals through tax cuts; on the other hand, it permits for tax increases in certain fields in order to optimize the structure of tax revenue. In short, it has always unequivocally been inherent in the concept of structural tax reduction that tax reduction operations should meet the taxation reform head-on (Gao Peiyong, 2011).

Regarding the direction of the taxation reform, particularly the reform aiming for tax structure optimization, we cannot talk about it without the recognition of our actual tax structure and the planned tax reform for the Twelfth Five-Year Plan period.

Let's look at the 2011 case. The statistic reports from the State Administration of Taxation (Department of Revenue Planning and Accounting, SAT, 2011) state over 70 percent of total tax revenue in 2011 came from turnover taxes, while under 30 percent was from non-turnover taxes (including the income tax). And 92.06 percent of taxes are paid by enterprises while only 7.94 percent are paid by individuals.

These figures deliver us two explicit facts in China. One is that over 70 percent of tax revenue comes from indirect taxes, which are levied on commodities as a component of their market prices and ultimately shifted to consumers through the pricing channel. The other is that over 90 percent of our tax revenue comes from the taxes paid by enterprises. Those taxes are usually squeezed into the commodity prices as a component of the production or operational cost, and are likely to be shifted through the pricing channel. In fact, most taxes in modern China are paid by corporate legal entities and incorporated into commodity prices. Those are two typical features of our actual tax operation pattern, which also reveal an imbalance between our prevailing tax structure and its actual tax revenue structure.

It's not strange to us that such a serious imbalance between our prevailing tax structure and our actual tax revenue structure has caused us many troubles in the process of our economic and social development. Besides, its drawbacks have become more and more prominent in the condition of global economic unrest.

First of all, highly proportioned and dosed indirect taxes are shifted or scattered to the whole society mainly in the disguise of commodity prices. These taxes indeed push up commodity prices in our real life, as they are closely associated. What's worse, when inflation pressure is high and the upward trend of prices continues – just like what happened last year – taxes and prices will be driven up in turn, and more uncertainties will affect our government's great efforts at price control. In some sense, China's taxes have already been turned into the unbearable heaviness of commodity prices.

Second, highly proportioned and dosed taxes are paid by various enterprises. Nominally, the tax burdens for various enterprises and even the total tax burden for Chinese enterprises are thus increased. Besides, the competitiveness of enterprises with varying sizes relies on their tax burdens. In fact, micro- and small-sized enterprises bear heavier tax burdens than medium- and large-sized enterprises. In some sense, China's taxes have already been turned into the unbearable heaviness for enterprises.

Third, given our excessive reliance on indirect taxes and corporate income taxes, it is difficult to redefine the payers of China's vast majority of taxes, which in fact are ultimately paid by our consumers. In addition, it distracts our government's attention, to a great extent, from other tax categories or items, and diverts our efforts from direct taxes represented by the income tax and property tax. It is indeed hard to exert the functions of modern taxes like regulating income distribution, bridging the wealth gap, etc.

Fourth, given the sharp differences between domestic and foreign tax systems, our excessive reliance on indirect taxes and corporate income taxes will fuel the prices of domestic commodities relative to foreign ones, thereby impairing the competitiveness of our commodities and enterprises in the global market, and it will result in varied prices of import and export commodities through export tax rebates. These consequences, of course, will give rise to or increase global trade friction at a time when American and European economic situations are quite unstable and trade protectionism is overwhelming.

Still, there are many such drawbacks. All of these have justified the position that China's current tax structure and its resulting revenue structure need to be adjusted without delay, just as does China's actual economic structure. The adjustment direction is self-evident. It is to decrease indirect taxes and increase direct taxes, and to decrease taxes paid by enterprises but increase taxes paid by individuals on the premise that China's macro tax burden is reduced to an appropriate level.

Based on the understanding, we deliberately wrote a passage into Section 3, Chapter 47 of the Outline of the Twelfth Five-Year Plan Draft (2011) in effect. It says: "We will improve the taxation system and enhance the construction of the taxation legal system under the guidelines of optimizing tax system structure, equalizing tax burdens, standardizing distribution relationship and improving allocation of taxing rights."

When discussing structural tax reductions against this background, we can reach the conclusion immediately that indirect taxes or turnover taxes paid by enterprises and shifted through the pricing channel should be and could be reduced in 2012 when proactive fiscal policy is dominant.

## Tax reductions targeted at VAT

Under China's existing tax structure, VAT, consumption tax, business tax and customs duty are categorized into indirect or turnover taxes. Except for customs duty which has its own features and is directly correlated with the foreign trade, proportion of the rest taxes is not equal. VAT share of total tax revenue is the highest among the three. In 2011, VAT revenue in China accounted for 37.75 percent of total tax revenue, and revenue from consumption tax and business tax accounted for 9.41 percent and 14.29 percent, respectively. Of course, we have different relief measures for these taxes.

As discussed previously, we will definitely give first priority to maximizing the effects of structural tax reductions as much as possible only if our government could afford to do so, given the existing economic situation and the necessity to continue implementing proactive fiscal policy. Now VAT takes a bigger share than any do other turnover taxes, and the pilot reform policy for the transformation from business tax to VAT has already been introduced. Eventually, business tax will be replaced by VAT. This trend is irreversible. Above all, the extended VAT revenue ratio will hit 50 percent unless additional supporting measures are launched. Consumption tax has its own special nature. It is levied on luxury merchandise as surtax. Increasing or decreasing the consumption tax has long been debated, and no consensus has been reached yet. Structural tax reductions are finally targeted at nothing but VAT.

The pilot program for the transformation from business tax to VAT initialized in Shanghai happens to carve out a way to structural tax reductions for us. This is very delightful. This proposal maximizes the effects of structural tax reductions, at least from the following three aspects:

First, the tax burdens for the involved industries will be reduced due to a decline of double taxation after the pilot reforms. The double taxation exists where business tax applies as it's nondeductible. This is one significant inborn limitation that VAT does not have. When VAT is gradually extended to the application scope of business tax, more business taxes levied on the involved industries will be changed to VAT; therefore, double taxation will be minimized.

Second, the tax burdens for the involved industries will be reduced due to an alleviation of imbalanced burdens of two taxes. Since the VAT reform started in 2009, the VAT burden, compared to the business tax burden, has already been mitigated. The drop of the VAT burden contrasts with a relative rise of the business tax burden. When VAT is gradually extended to the application scope of business tax, more business taxes levied on the involved industries will be changed to VAT; therefore, the imbalance conflict will be relieved.

Finally, as VAT is gradually extended to the application scope of business tax, two new lower VAT rates of 11 percent and 6 percent are added into the current VAT brackets where 17 percent and 13 percent are the standard and the lower rates, respectively. The overall or average VAT burden is thus reduced. Furthermore, the decline of the overall or average VAT burden becomes an irresistible trend as the whole taxation reform proceeds. It implies a possibility that the future VAT brackets and rates will be more inclusive and lower.

What delights us more is that the efficient tax relief reform is not limited to Shanghai. Any other areas could apply for this pilot program. Beijing, Jiangsu Province and Shenzhen have submitted their applications so far. It is estimated that tax reductions resulting from the full transition from business tax to VAT will be increasing as the pilot program was started in Shanghai in 2012 and then expands nationwide.

We can assume, unlike any other previous tax reforms, that any slight move on VAT, the biggest tax in China, may affect the whole taxation system. As the pilot program of the transition from business tax to VAT is extended nationwide, significant reforms on VAT and even all other turnover taxes will be launched for the objectives of tax relief and an improvement of the turnover tax system. After that, direct taxes represented by taxes on property and personal incomes will be reformed, and then a comprehensive tax reform will be promoted to optimize our tax structure.

## Spending increase centered on improving peoples' livelihoods

We mentioned before that proactive fiscal policy could be operated from two clues all along – increased spending and tax reduction. Among all arrangements of the 2012 proactive fiscal policy, we cannot underestimate or neglect the spending increase plans despite our focus on structural tax reduction. But 2012 spending increase plans are just playing a supporting role, different from what they used to play. After we have come to a conclusion favoring tax cuts, our focus shifts to the other clue: spending increase.

Regarding spending increase, the main carrier of fiscal expansion is shifted from "spending increase" to "tax reduction", because what we value most is a balance between one goal of steady economic growth and the other of economic structural adjustment, mentioned before. Actually, to achieve such a balance, we can set about selecting projects for additional investments and adjusting the expenditure structure, apart from the main carrier shift.

Given that the current expansionary operations could be done in no hurry, given that stabilizing prices remains our top priority, and given that the two objectives of steady growth and structure adjustment should be compatible with each other – especially the history of sacrificing structure adjustment for steady growth should not be repeated, 2012 spending increase moves should be centered on improving people's livelihood. We will increase financial investment and accomplish major tasks that are directly related to the people's livelihood improvement (Xinhua News Agency, 2011). In other words, the focus of spending increase will be shifted from investment in the past to boosting consumption demand at an appropriate time.

To be specific, in addition to investment structure optimization, our most important work is to boost consumption demand by increasing investments in a series of projects that aim to improve peoples' livelihoods. The important projects in need of special attention are: implementing the minimum wage system in order raise low-income earners' labor remuneration; boosting farmers' incomes; basically achieving a full coverage by the social endowment insurance system for rural residents and social endowment insurance for non-working urban residents, and raising subsistence allowances for both urban and rural residents, benefits for entitled groups and basic pensions for enterprise retirees; establishing a safeguard mechanism for positive growth and payment of salaries of enterprise employees; increasing financial subsidies in order to raise incomes for both urban and rural residents, especially the lower- and lowest-income groups, and effectively relieve the burdens of the poverty-stricken on education, medical services and housing; strongly supporting affordable government-subsidized housing projects, etc.

It's anticipated that 2012 proactive fiscal policy will fit in with the current global economic situation and coordinate with our macroeconomic arrangements only if it focuses on structural tax reduction operations and is complemented by a series of spending increase operations which aim at improving peoples' livelihoods – only if our revenue and expenditure suit very well and echo each other.

(Originally published in *Finance & Trade Economics*, Vol. 2, 2012)

## References

Department of Revenue Planning and Accounting, SAT, *Monthly Tax Revenue Express*, December 2011

Editorial Committee of China's Finance Year Book: *Finance Year Book of China*, China State Finance Magazine, 2002

Gao Peiyong, Structural Tax Reduction Shall Meet the Taxation Reform Head on, *China Financial and Economic News*, December 27, 2011

Jin Renqing, *Comments on Chinese Contemporary Tax Revenue*, People's Publishing House, 2002

Li Yang, Current Global Economic Situation and Macroeconomic Policies, *Chinese Social Sciences Today*, November 15, 2011

Ministry of Finance, Report on 2010 Central and Local Budget Implementation and 2011 Central and Local Budget Draft, *People's Daily*, March 17, 2011

Outline of the Twelfth Five-year Plan of National Economic and Social Development of the People's Republic of China, *People's Daily*, March 16, 2011

Wen Jiabao, Corruption and Inflation Could Have an Adverse Impact on Social Stability in China, *China Economic Net*, September 14, 2011

Xinhua News Agency, The CEWC Held in Beijing on December 12 to 14, *People's Daily*, December 14, 2011

# 10 Macroeconomic policy options against the background of a complicated and volatile economy

## Preface

After an overall evaluation of the global economic situation, the 2012 CEWC decided to continue to implement proactive fiscal policy and prudent monetary policy. At that time, our "proactive and prudent" macroeconomic policy package that lasted for two years came to its third year.

Since 2008 when this round of global financial crisis broke out, spread and changed, our macroeconomic policy package has undergone two types: a "proactive and moderately loose" package, and a "proactive and prudent" package. The former refers to a proactive fiscal policy and a moderately loose monetary policy, implemented from 2008–2010; the latter, a proactive fiscal policy and a prudent monetary policy, implemented from 2011 to now.

When the Asian financial crisis struck in 1998, it was the first time for China to apply proactive fiscal policy with a complement of so-called "appropriate" monetary policy. It was a "proactive and appropriate" package. Three years later when our economy turned for the better, the appropriate monetary policy was replaced by a prudent one in 2001. The policy package we used was turned into the "proactive and prudent" consisting of proactive fiscal policy and prudent monetary policy. In 2005, we substituted prudent fiscal policy for the proactive one, and we applied the so-called "double prudent" policy package, consisting of prudent fiscal and monetary policies, until 2008.

This basic track how our macroeconomic policy package has moved by far indicates several facts as follows:

- Unlike the "expansionary", "tight" and "neutral" macroeconomic policies in the textbooks of economics, those so-called "proactive", "appropriate", or "prudent" and "moderately loose" policies in our country have a strong literary flavor and no explicit connotation or denotation of policy definitions.

  (Xiang Huaicheng, 2002)

- Even now people get used to identifying proactive with expansionary, prudent with neutral, moderately tight with tight in policy concepts, but we still are left with enough room to maneuver our macroeconomic policy. For example, a proactive policy doesn't have to contain expansionary contents. It's likely to be manipulated prudently under the "proactive" name. Likewise, a "prudent" policy on paper doesn't necessarily have neutral elements, but is likely to be expansionary or tight in fact.

• The formation of the macroeconomic policy package is certainly associated with the changes of economic situation; however, a macroeconomic policy under the same name or package is likely to imply different practical elements, even significant adjustments or changes. For example, a policy package implemented in 2011 was then continued in 2012 and 2013, but it doesn't mean all policy arrangements imposed in 2011 were duplicated in 2012 and 2013. Significantly different contents might exist in the economic aggregate and structure under the banner of "continuous implementation".

Those factors add difficulties to our understanding and implementation of macroeconomic theories in reality. The only way to address such difficulties or problems is to read carefully between the lines and understand the practical contents, and then try to restore the real picture of our macroeconomic policy arrangements based on the changes of our national and worldwide conditions.

## Moving forward in economic upheaval: China's economic trend in 2013

Incorporating as many of the various performances or factors of the current global economic conditions as possible into the whole picture, we can conclude that our economy will move forward through upheavals along the 2012 track despite of a series of uncertainties.

Such a conclusion is drawn from the following evidence:

### *The global economy is undergoing a very miserable and relatively long process of deep transition and adjustment*

People once described this particular crisis as "unprecedented like it's never occurred in a hundred years". At the very beginning, its particularity refers more to its spread range and effect depth, and of course its duration. In other words, although people realized that this crisis is totally different from previous ones, they generally regarded it as a periodic crisis and still took specific measures against cyclical crisis. Consequently, both the developed economies, like the EU, USA and Japan, and the emerging economies represented by BRICS countries – despite they had manipulated massive and excessive economic incentives since they were trapped into this crisis and most announced signs of recovery and even achieved a recovery – have not successfully moved back to the track of cyclical rebound yet as usual or as expected, and in fact have been experiencing continual ups and downs. To this day, the developed economies are still sluggish, their debt crises rise one after another, and the emerging economies are slowing down in succession; thus, the global economy grows at a low rate.

Seemingly the fundamental reason for this lies in the fact that this global financial crisis is not simply cyclical in the traditional sense, but is combined with both structural and cyclical factors, with even more attributed to the structural factor. Just on account of the economic structure adjustment around the world, the global economy has to go through a very miserable and relatively long process of deep transition and adjustment, thereby moving in a track of constant upheavals.

Beyond doubt, it is impossible for China to keep itself out of this process of deep transition and adjustment. The global economies are inextricably interwoven in the condition of thorough change and development of economic globalization. It's like a bit of me in you and a bit of you in me. No nation or region could hardly get away from the risks once global economies have unrest. More importantly, the Chinese economy is naturally a part of the global economic system. Anything happening in any corner of the world matters to any other nation and region in the world; no one could stay alone (Li Yang, 2012). It means China's economy will run into a great number of uncertainties as it moves forward.

### *China's economy is under the pressure of structural adjustment and has also slowed down its growth*

Actually earlier before this crisis, the contradictions of unbalanced, uncoordinated and unsustainable economic structure in China exposed themselves completely and were acknowledged by people. Against this background, we started a series of unprecedented actions aimed at adjusting our economic structure. However, this round of global financial crisis interrupts our process, and we have to suspend our efforts to adjust economic structure and turn to concentrate on the measures aimed at maintaining growth.

After several years of expansionary operations where government investment is expanded for the exchange of economic growth, the "extensive" expansion has increasingly more adverse effects on our economic structure. We are depressed to find that the long lasting structural contradiction in our economy is not weakened but reinforced now, compared to what it was before the crisis. Meanwhile, as our industrialization has entered into its middle and later periods – during which demographic dividends are reduced and labor cost is rising – our adjustment weights towards the vigorous development of the service industry. It inevitably slows down the growth of social labor productivity and of the overall economy. On the one hand, all these make the contradiction of economic structure imbalance evolve into a contradiction of relative excess capacity; on the other hand, the downturned economy and the relative excess capacity interwoven closely become more challenging for our economic development.

When we recognize that economic structure adjustment is surely accompanied by economic instability and the efforts to change the mode of economic development won't be successful in the short run, we cannot but accept one basic fact that the Chinese economy will not only fall into recession but also undergo constant upheavals. In fact, after reviewing the track of our economic growth that started after this global financial crisis, we discover that our economy has already slowed down and vibrated.

### China is confronted with an economic upheaval that is the sign of recovery rather than another crisis, after all

Against the backdrop of the complicated and volatile global economic situation, our economy moves upward for sure despite economic upheaval. It should be noted that it doesn't shift its upward trend. The upheaval that our economy is confronted with is actually a sign of recovery rather than another crisis, after all. In other words, our economy will neither have a V-shaped recovery as its growth rate hits its bottom, rises again back to 9 percent, 10 percent and then keeps even higher, nor will it show a so-called W- or L-shaped recovery as its growth rate either hits the bottom, recovers briefly and then hits another bottom, or hovers at the bottom for long without any signs of recovery. In 2013 and some future period, our economy is likely to grow at a rate (such as 7–8 percent) that is a little bit lower than the previous rate (average 9.8 percent in last 30 years) and enters an era of so-called medium growth.

Apart from those factors, there are at still some other reasons that are worthy to be discussed. They are as follows:

First, the track of this global financial crisis up to now reveals that the most difficult period for global economies was from the end of 2008 to the beginning of 2009. Comparing the global economic conditions in the current period of upheavals to that in the most difficult period, we discover that – no matter in the developed economies like the EU, USA and Japan or in the emerging economies represented by BRICS countries – the economic growth has not yet dropped to the level of 2008 and 2009, despite those unsatisfactory economic indices. As long as the economy stays above the level from the end of 2008 to the beginning of 2009, its fluctuations and upheavals suggest a revival ahead.

Second, against the background that the world is caught in the all-around and profound structural contradiction, the developed economies like the EU, USA and Japan, although finding it hard to get rid of constant upheavals in the short term, are not absolutely incurable and cornered. Such an argument is well justified by a series of events happening to the US fiscal cliff and the European sovereign-debt crisis.

Third, more importantly, after several years of operations against the global financial crisis, we are not as lost or in panic as we were at the break of the crisis. We used to resort to excessive and temporarily effective solutions, but now we have experience and have become seasoned and are able to figure out some solutions and rules to fight against such special cases as this global financial crisis. Our macro control art becomes more matured and macroeconomic policy arrangements make more sense when we are faced with new challenges and opportunities.

## Macroeconomic policy: directed towards dual effect and multiple objectives at once

### *2013 expansionary measures different from the previous*

Obviously, when the global financial crisis tends to last for long and our economy moves upward despite of the unrest, our macroeconomic policy – no matter under the name of a "proactive and moderately loose" package or a "proactive and prudent" package – is inclined to be expansionary in general. The "proactive and prudent" package in 2013, of course, belongs to the expansionary macro control measures on the whole.

As noted, this round of expansionary measures has been implemented for five years since 2008. After that period, the 2013 measures vary from the previous in at least three aspects:

First, the efficacy of expansionary measures is declining, according to the law of diminishing marginal utility. It means the excessive and massive economic expansionary measures won't be as effective as they were in 2008 and 2009.

Second, as said before, when expansionary economic policy functions according to its own law, the "extensive" expansion has increasingly more adverse effects on our economic structure. We are now under greater pressure than we were before the crisis, as the task of structural adjustment is heavier and more urgent than it was before.

Third, as the global economy keeps up and down, and the serious imbalanced, inharmonious and unsustainable problems are emerging, more and more facts have proven that a recovery in a real sense will never come unless the existing economic structure changes. For this reason, we have to intensify strategic adjustment of economic structure and completely transform our economic development mode in order to get our economy back to the track of healthy and sustainable development.

On the one hand, it means, even though "the global economy will continue to grow at a low rate", "the contradiction between the downturn economy and relative excess capacity is intensified", and our macroeconomic policy stays expansionary in general, we can neither simply apply excessive and massive economic expansionary measures as we did in 2008 and 2009, nor achieve the expected economic growth at the price of structural adjustment. On the other hand, it means, in order to obtain high-quality, efficient and sustainable economic growth, or healthy and sustainable economic growth during the process of constant transition of economic development mode and constant optimization of economic structure, we have to balance multiple objectives – steady growth, structural adjustment, price control and risk prevention – and find a harmonious and coordinated solution to regulate a counter-cyclical economy and promote structural adjustment.

### *Integrating counter-cyclical regulation with structural adjustment promotion*

In the sense of conventional economics, macroeconomic policies are usually used as a counter-cyclical tool. Its macrocontrol effects can be summarized as "leaning against the wind" in that the expansionary measures are taken in economic recession while the tight measures are taken in the inflationary times. In our history, at least after the Asian financial crisis in 1998, macroeconomic policies in different periods are all made for counter-cyclical regulation, no matter if they were a "proactive fiscal and appropriate monetary" policy package, or a "proactive and prudent" package, or a "proactive and moderately loose" package, or a "dual prudent" package in recent years.

Our macroeconomic policies used to play an exclusive role of counter-cyclical regulation, but the 2013 policy is directed at both counter-cyclical regulation and structural adjustment promotion. In other words, the 2013 policy must have the effects of both counter-cyclical regulation and structural adjustment promotion. It has thoughtful causes and considerations.

First, this round of global financial crisis is an outcome of both periodic and structural factors, and mainly caused by imbalanced economic structure. Neither the global economy nor our economy could be recovered in the real sense and then go back to the normal track of the healthy and sustainable development unless its economic structure is adjusted.

Second, now our economy is trapped in a vicious cycle where the downward pressure on economic growth and the production overcapacity contradict with each other. Macro-control measures against either one will lead to ineffective allevia-tion, unless they are applied to both at the same time. As long as a two-pronged strategy is developed to have an effect on both counter-cyclical regulation and structural economic adjustment, the macroeconomic policy arrangements will finally fit in with our economic reality.

Third, in order to avoid altering economic structure during the anti-crisis pro-cess, or not gain the anti-crisis goals at the price of economic structure alteration, almost the only option left for us at present is to start from industrial structure adjustment and finally promote economic growth with structural adjustment or obtain the goal that economic growth is compatible with structure adjustment by addressing production overcapacity and relieving economic downward pressure.

### *Realizing multiple objectives including "steady growth, structural adjustment, price control and risk prevention"*

In this anti-crisis fight, our macroeconomic policy was initially targeted at "main-taining growth". When it overrode any other tasks, we could concentrate our resources with determination and spare no efforts to pursue it. Later when the economic situation was eased and changed, we substituted "steady growth" for "maintaining growth", and also then supplemented additional objectives of mac-roeconomic policies into the original bracket. Besides "steady growth", "price control" was added due to the inflation driven by excess liquidity and then "struc-tural adjustment" was added due to the increasingly serious issues concerning economic structure. Up to now, a series of so-called objectives have taken shape. The hidden risks of financial sectors will become increasingly visible in 2013 as a variety of debts that were borrowed through anti-crisis measures a few years ago are due in succession. It becomes an important task of the macro-control enhance-ment and improvement to defend the bottom line that no systematic or regional financial risks should break out. "Risk prevention" is thereupon added into the objective bracket of our macroeconomic policy. The triple target evolves into a quadruple target, consisting of "steady growth, price control, structural adjustment and risk prevention".

When we have more than one objective, such as three, four or even more, we have to de-concentrate our macro-control resources. Macro-control operations are anchored in our attempts to attack and conquer all fronts at once. Actually it tells us, due to our dispersed forces, that our macro-control actions in 2013 should and have to be flexible to achieve steady growth, structural adjustment, price control and risk prevention successfully. It also means, given the pressing necessity for steady growth and given that steady growth is required to be placed in a more important position, we can spare no efforts or devote our most energy to steady growth like we used to, but we must achieve or balance several objectives at once. Let me draw an inappropriate analogy. It seems like a child, who is disciplined by several adults with diversified values, has to be obedient to everyone and is afraid of displeasing anyone. As a result, the effective room for macro control is compressed to a great extent on one hand, and the objective priority or the major force of our macro control is hard to determine on the other hand. Either side that is under greater pressure (in more difficult situations) will receive more resources allocated through macro control.

Our macroeconomic policy is directed to "dual effect" rather than "single effect" and "multiple objectives" rather than "single one" at once. The economy has no choice but to wander between the dual effect and multiple objectives due to their containment. Perhaps this is the best description about how our macroeconomic policy decides its way out.

## A "proactive and prudent" package: fiscal policy takes the lead

Our proactive fiscal policy and prudent monetary policy, although as parts of expansionary moves in general, are surely endowed with different roles and tasks. Given that most developed economies like the EU, USA and Japan are introducing a new series of quantitative easing policies one after another, the major currencies worldwide will be devalued due to extra money printed, and the pressure on potential inflation and asset bubble will be increased, eventually resulting in an overflow effect on our economy; given the accumulated and increased hidden risks of our financial sectors, new local governments are likely impulsive to establish new local financing platforms after they take office; and given that the previous inflationary pressure caused by excess liquidity is not relieved yet, a new round of inflationary pressure input from the outside and created from the inside is being generated. Against such background, the functional room of monetary policy is therefore constrained or compressed to a great extent, so that we have to devote our greatest efforts at price control and risk prevention. It means the proactive fiscal policy takes the lead of all expansionary moves in 2013.

Common sense tells us as an expansionary macro control move, the proactive fiscal policy – in whatever background or from whatever perspective – will be implemented in three specific aspects: namely deficit increase, tax cut and expenditure expansion. In other words, to implement fiscal expansion, we shall start from deficit increase, tax cut and expenditure expansion. The 2013 proactive fiscal policy is not an exception.

### Deficit increase

Deficit increase is very necessary because it's indeed an essential condition for the implementation of fiscal expansion moves, but deficit is not bound to result in expansion. Basically, whether the economy leads to expansion and what extent it expands directly depends on the scale of fiscal deficit and its marginal effect. The expansion effect of fiscal deficit is great as long as its scale is large. If fiscal deficit in this year is more than that in the last year, it means the fiscal policy implemented in this year probably intends to be expansionary; if the same, it means it intends to be neutral; if less, it means to be tight.

To implement fiscal expansion, the 2013 fiscal deficit will be increased over the 2012 deficit. The 2012 fiscal budgetary deficit amounted to 1.07 trillion Yuan, including 800 billion Yuan offset by treasury bonds and 270 billion Yuan by the Central Budget Stabilization Fund. It is estimated that the increment of the fiscal deficit covered by debt financing will be hundreds of billions of Yuan, considering: (1) the fiscal revenue growth is probably reduced due to the negative effect of economy slowdown in 2013; (2) the fiscal revenue and expenditure contradiction gets worse due to fiscal expansion implementation and increased spending on other aspects; (3) more borrowing is needed to make up the deficit as the available stock of the Central Budget Stabilization Fund is less than it was and as the 2012 excessive fiscal revenue is relatively reduced. Including the deficit covered by the Central Budget Stabilization Fund, the whole fiscal budgetary deficit is likely to break through 1.2 trillion Yuan and hit the record of 1.3 trillion billion Yuan.

### Tax cut

A fixed amount of fiscal budgetary deficit leaves us to two fiscal measures, namely tax cut and expenditure expansion. In other words, a fixed amount of fiscal deficit can support either tax cut or expenditure expansion, or both, depending on the expansion effects of proactive fiscal policy. Our common sense also tells us that given the multiplicative difference of tax cuts and expenditure, generally speaking, expenditure expansion has greater and more direct expansionary effect than tax cuts; tax cuts have less and more indirect effect than expenditure expansion. Given the current package of our macroeconomic policies that intend to take dual effect and obtain multiple objectives, and given that strengths and weakness of all aspects are weighed up, it's believed that the 2013 proactive fiscal policy should and must focus on structural tax cuts.

Why we should concentrate on structural tax cuts rather than public spending expansion? The reason is tax cuts, as the main carrier of expansionary measures, are to increase private disposable incomes rather than direct public investment to achieve economic expansion. It helps achieving steady economic growth by counter-cyclical regulation on one hand, and more importantly, it hands over more decision-making powers to the market on the other hand. As a result, the fundamental role of the market is played in resource allocation to a greater extent and in a larger scope, and the "extensive economy" trap caused by direct government investment can be avoided. Eventually, the proactive fiscal policy takes better effect on promoting structural adjustment. In this regard, actually since 2012, particularly the second half of that year, structural tax cuts have evolved into the main carrier of the proactive fiscal policy. In 2013 its role won't and shouldn't have a major change. In addition, due to the traction of dual effect and multiple objectives, the effect of the structural tax cut on fiscal expansion will be highlighted and even determine the success of this round of macro-control measures.

In summary, at least half of the 2013 fiscal budgetary deficit should be used to promote structural tax cuts.

### *Expenditure expansion*

Beyond doubt, public expenditure expansion is indispensable in implementing fiscal expansion. In our previous patterns of macroeconomic policies, the measures to expand public spending did have great achievements as the carrier. It's the measures to expand public spending that we were able to first get on the upturn track when the global financial crisis was raging. However, given the changed macroeconomic conditions and given that our macroeconomic policy package has had major adjustments, and especially given that the necessity for both counter-cyclical regulation and structural adjustment promotion has been increasingly urgent, the measures to expand public spending have to be constrained in 2013. Our governments at all levels should economize by strictly controlling regular expenditures and spending money on important items that must be done. Moreover, as far as the public investment that should be increased is concerned, our governments at all levels should focus on those infrastructure constructions that are fundamental, non-redundant and benefit peoples' livelihoods for long while increasing and guiding private investment. It means that in the 2013 fiscal budgetary deficit, the part that is allocated for government spending should be less than that in the previous years, or at least less than the part allocated for structural tax cuts.

## BT to VAT reform: main battlefield of macro-control operations

As the main carrier of proactive fiscal policy, the advancing path and specific arrangements of structural tax cuts become definitely the most beautiful landscape in the pattern of our 2013 macroeconomic policies. It's not only because structural tax cuts happen to be the compromise solution that has taken all factors into consideration in the tug of war, as today's macro control must play double roles to obtain multiple objectives, but also because structural tax cuts are an initiative that can win the approval of most Chinese at present among many macroeconomic policy options. In some sense, now structural tax cuts have already become the main battlefield of macro-control operations in China.

To popularize the structural tax cuts, there are of course many options. For example, it seems that 18 taxes in our current taxation system can receive cuts. However, if the current taxation system is aligned with the Twelfth Five-Year Plan, or if it is just for a balanced system of tax revenue, the structural tax cut should undoubtedly emphasize indirect taxes over indirect taxes and major indirect taxes with larger shares over the marginal ones with smaller shares. Because of that, the 2013 CEWC set policy "to improve the structural tax cut policies in alignment with the tax reform".

To be detailed, under our existing taxation system, the major indirect taxes with larger revenue shares are value-added tax (VAT), business tax (BT) and consumption tax. In 2012 they were 39.8 percent, 15.6 percent and 9.0 percent of revenues, respectively. If they were placed on the chessboard of the whole taxation reform and then aligned with the current progress of the taxation reform, it would be found that only VAT is the best target for the structural tax cut. The reasons are obvious, as follows:

First of all, the taxation reform that is designed in the Twelfth Five-Year Plan is to complete the transformation from BT to VAT step by step. It's irreversible that BT will be eventually replaced by VAT. By the end of the twelfth five-year period, it will be included in the VAT system.

Second, consumption tax is usually levied on luxuries and commodities that consume energy and resources. Any cut on consumption tax involves national revenue distribution policies and energy saving policies, on which a consensus is always hard to reach. Hence, consumption tax has to be treated very carefully.

Third, VAT takes a larger share than any other tax in our current tax system. Now it's the biggest tax in China. Any change on VAT, even a mild change, will tremendously affect the overall tax revenue, but a VAT cut will achieve maximum relief effect.

Therefore, reducing VAT or to giving first priority to VAT cut is almost the only right choice for us to carry out the structural tax cut.

Encouragingly, the BT to VAT (B2V) pilot program itself, carried out now in Shanghai, is a structural tax cut move that has the largest scale and affects the widest range. It's a good stepping stone for further VAT relief. The reasons are as follows:

- When BT is gradually replaced by VAT, the double taxation which exists where business tax applies as it's nondeductible will be minimized, as the involved industries are included into the application scope of VAT. As a result, the original tax burdens for those industries will be reduced after the VAT reform.
- When BT is gradually replaced by VAT, the VAT burden drops with a relative rise of the business tax burden. The conflict of unbalanced tax burdens caused by the VAT reform will be relieved as the involved industries are

included into the application scope of VAT. As a result, the original tax burdens for those industries will be reduced after the VAT reform.

- When BT is gradually replaced by VAT, and two additional lower VAT rates of 11 percent and 6 percent are added into our current VAT brackets, the average VAT rate and the whole VAT burden will be reduced over the previous configuration, where two higher rates of 17 percent and 13 percent apply.

In fact, the B2V pilot program carried out in Shanghai over the past year has achieved more tax relief than expected. Given that the pilot VAT program has extended to Beijing, Jiangsu, Anhui, Fujian, Guangdong, Tianjin, Zhejiang and Hubei, and given that the pilot program will eventually extend through the whole country and cover all service sectors, the most conservative case is VAT reform, which is estimated to cut taxes by hundreds of billions of Yuan.

In 2013, we should focus on the structural tax cut, the main carrier, and target at VAT for tax relief. The specific implementation options for us are as follows:

Option 1 is to accelerate extending the B2V pilot program to a wider scope. The wider the scope the B2V pilot program extends to, the more vertical industries it involves and the larger scale effect the structural tax cut will achieve. Surely it's helpful for us to achieve structural tax relief if we concentrate on the pilot areas and industrial sectors of the B2V reform and then take feasible and effective moves to drive the B2V reform forward.

Option 2 is to lower the standard VAT rates in addition to the extension. If we extend the VAT system that was designed based on the operating features of the manufacturing business to the service business, we should neither neglect the operating features of the service business before making adaptive adjustment on one hand, nor disintegrate both manufacturing and service businesses before remaking system arrangements on the other hand. We should consider the needs of both industries and value the long-term development by extending the application scope and lowering the VAT rates as well. Lowering the existing overall standard VAT rates will provide material relief of the actual average VAT burden.

(Originally published in *Finance & Trade Economics*, Vol. 2, 2013)

## References

Gao Peiyong, Boosting Structural Tax Cut: Scale Definition, Target Selection and Specific Path, *Guang Ming Daily*, August 13, 2012

Li Yang, Improving Efficiency Is the Key to Transformational Development, from *2013 China's Economic Situation Analysis and Forecast*, Social Sciences Academic Press, 2012

Xiang Huaicheng, Proactive Fiscal Policy Is Political Wisdom, *China Times*, August 17, 2002

Xinhua News Agency, The CEWC Held in Beijing on December 12 to 14, *People's Daily*, December 16, 2012

# 11 Remain calm in the face of declining growth of financial revenue

While China's economy goes into new stage of development, its financial revenue tends to slow down, and all of the society pays much attention to it. In a sense, it is a hot topic accompanying with the change of economy in China. Much discussion and repercussions at least indicate that it is a strange issue. Many young people may never experience it and many old ones may haven't experienced it for a long time. Since it is a comparatively strange but very realistic and objective economic phenomenon, it should be studied quickly and deeply by new thoughts from new views.

## The judgment of the situation of financial revenue has direct correlation to the reference system

Judgment about the situation of financial revenue has direct correlation to the reference system (reference standard) used. Different reference systems will induce different even totally different conclusions.

For example, the total financial revenue in China from January to August this year was 8.9027 trillion Yuan. For the analysis based on this data in China, the "past" growth of financial revenue was always taken as reference. However, since the "past" may be a long history or short, the time range should be confirmed. Different time ranges will lead to different conclusions.

The growth rate of financial revenue in China this year is 8.1 percent. If the same period in the last year is considered the "past", we will find that, comparing with the growth rate of 10.8 percent from January to August last year, the growth rate this year decreases 2.7 percent.

If the past 10 years is considered the "past", we will find that, compared with the growth rate of 22.39 percent from 2003–2012, the growth rate of financial revenue this year decreases 14.29 percent.

If the past 19 years is considered the "past", we will find that, comparing with the growth rate of 20.2 percent from 1994–2012, the growth rate of financial revenue this year decreases 12.1 percent.

Further, if the past 34 years is considered the "past", we will find that, comparing with the growth rate of 15.2 percent from 1979–2012, the growth rate of financial revenue this year decreases 7.1 percent.

If the period lasting 15 years from the beginning of reform and opening up to the beginning of tax reform is considered the "past", we will find that, comparing with the growth rate of 8.94 percent from 1979–1993, the growth rate of financial revenue this year just decreases 0.84 percent.

It can be seen that, accompanying with the change of reference system of "past", the judgment about the growth rate of financial revenue this year changes greatly. Taking the 10 years with "super-high growth rate" (2003–2012) as reference, it will naturally lead to the conclusion that the current growth rate of financial revenue in China decreases greatly and its situation is severe; taking the 19 years with "high growth rate" (1994–2012) as reference, the current growth rate of financial revenue in China decreases but the situation is not so severe; taking the 34 years since the reform and opening-up policy (2003–2012) as reference, the current growth rate of financial revenue in China decreases to a single-digit growth rate that can be accepted. Further, taking the 15 years of early reform and opening-up policy as reference, the current growth rate of financial revenue in China decreases so little that it can be ignored.

It indicates that for the judgment about current situation of financial revenue in China, it is unnecessary and improper to worry about the current financial revenue, but one should take a comparatively calm and optimistic attitude.

## The declining growth of financial revenue is an economic phenomenon in line with the law

Reviewing the declining growth of financial revenue against the background of a long process of history, especially the special background of international financial crisis, the following facts can't be ignored.

It is a well-known basic rule that economy decides finance. With the reforms of more than 30 years, China's economy has gone into a new stage of development. The decrease of demographic dividend, the increase of labor cost and the adjustment of industry policy which strives to develop service industry now unavoidably cause the declining growth of both social labor productivity and economy. In other words, while high-speed economic growth turns to moderate-speed economic growth, the growth of financial revenue naturally declines accordingly. This is the first point.

The current international financial crisis is not pure periodic crisis in the conventional sense, but the crisis is interwoven with structural factors and periodic factors, and structural factors are even considered to be the main cause. Such factors are caused by the adjustment of global economic structure, and the economy in China is interwoven with global economy deeply. The task to adjust economic structure in China is very heavy and it has to experience a tough and comparatively long process of deep transition and adjustment. In this process, with continuous economic upheaval and slowdown, it will also experience continuous financial revenue upheaval and slowdown. This is the second point.

The continuous high-speed – even super-speed – growth of financial revenue started in 1994. Before that year, the growth rate of financial revenue declined continuously for years. The revenue increased for one year, then decreased in the next year; decreased in one year, then increased. The financial revenue tracking the "V" curve for the last 30 years indicates that the continuous high-speed growth of financial revenue is to a large extent the correction for continuous declining growth of financial revenue before, and it is the compensation for the declining growth before. Since the continuous high-speed growth of financial revenue is a kind of compensation, it will not be endless. Once the compensation reaches a certain level, it must come back to normal track. This is the third point.

The continuous high-speed growth of financial revenue since 1994 appeared after the tax reforms of that year. To a large extent, it can be thought as the product of tax reform in 1994, and it is a reform dividend. Since it is a reform dividend, the dividend effect can't continue for a long time. By the law of diminishing returns, when the dividend effect continues for a period, it will diminish. It means that the continuous high-speed growth of financial revenue, especially the growth which is much higher than economic growth, is just a special phenomenon at certain stage of development. Only the growth of financial revenue matching the economic growth is normal growth in economic life. This is the fourth point.

The subject of financial revenue in China is tax revenue. In the current tax system, more than 70 percent of the tax revenue is collected by indirect taxes including value-added tax, business tax, and consumption tax. This pattern of tax revenue of "one-sided indirect tax" means that most of the tax revenue in China will be one of the factors constituting the price, and it is attached to price. Because it is tied with the price of goods and services, it will shift accompanying with a change of price, and slight change of price may induce severe turbulence of tax revenue. Thus, on condition of high-speed economic growth, the growth of tax revenue may be higher than economic growth; when the economic growth slows down or is lower than the past, the growth of tax revenue may be lower than economic growth. Therefore, if the current tax system and the pattern of tax revenue decided by it remain unchanged, great declining growth of both tax revenue and financial revenue induced by economic downturn is expected. This is the fifth point.

The declining growth of current financial revenue is not only the reality that has to be accepted, but also the result caused by the law of economic development. To some extent, it is the inevitable reflect of economy on financial revenue during the period of deep transition and adjustment; thus, it should be accepted by a normal mind.

## From macro perspective, the financial revenue is hardly severe

The previous analysis is based on data about public financial revenue and is calculated according to general budget scope. The more complex problem is that, in current China, public financial revenue or general budgetary revenue doesn't equal government revenue. Besides public financial revenue, there are several kinds of government revenue: governmental fund budgetary revenue, social security budgetary revenue, and state-owned capital operation budgetary revenue.

Taking the budget data in 2013 as an example, for the revenue and expenditure including the four kinds of budgetary revenue above, the proportion of public financial budgetary revenue is only about 65 percent. And the other three kinds of budgetary revenue are on the high side of about 35 percent. It means that the macro analysis on declining growth of financial revenue can't be limited to the scope of public financial budgetary revenue, but should be extended to "full coverage" including the four kinds of government revenue.

Once the analysis extends to governmental fund budgetary revenue, social security budgetary revenue, and state-owned capital operation budgetary revenue, it will be totally different from the analysis which only covers public financial budgetary revenue.

Take the governmental fund budgetary revenue and social security budgetary revenue which can be supported by data as example. According to the Ministry of Finance, from January to June, the national governmental fund budgetary revenue is 2.1061 trillion Yuan, increases of 587 billion Yuan and 38.6 percent, comparing with the same term last year. The social security budgetary revenue is 1.5276 trillion Yuan, which increases 15.6 percent. Comparing with the growth rate of public financial revenue in the same term (10.8 percent), the two kinds of government revenue above are 27.8 percent and 4.8 percent higher, respectively. From the perspective of 2 government revenue calculated according to "full coverage", once one decreases, the other will increase during the period of institutional transition; this special phenomenon indicates that if we only analyze the public financial revenue calculated according to general scope of budgetary revenue and expenditure to judge the financial situation, it is possible to make the conclusion that the situation is severe. However, if we analyze the government revenue covering all the four kinds of revenue calculated according to "full coverage", the current financial situation in China is hardly severe.

From another perspective, beyond the restriction of vertical self-comparison, the international horizontal comparison can help to understand it deeply.

Taking the representative countries and regions in 2012 as example, the growth rate of financial revenue in Organization for Economic Co-operation and Development (OECD) countries such as Australia is 8.54 percent, 4.27 percent in Austria, 3.54 percent in Canada, 5.85 percent in France, 5.59 percent in Germany, 2.1 percent in Japan, 0.54 percent in UK, 5.21 percent in US, 4.52 percent in Belgium, −1.29 percent in Denmark, 1.55 percent in Finland, −5.6 percent in Greece, 1.71 percent in Holland, 8.05 percent in Iceland, 1.44 percent in Ireland, 6.57 percent in Norway, −12.54 percent in Portugal, 0.6 percent in Spain, 2.1 percent in Sweden, −0.4 percent in Switzerland and 2.47 percent in Italy. And the growth rate of financial revenue in emerging market economies and surrounding countries such as India is 0.04 percent, 0.03 percent in Russia, −2.16 percent in Singapore, and 2.56 percent in Taiwan.

No matter if it takes the growth rate of financial revenue in developed OECD countries as reference, or if it takes the emerging market economies or the surrounding countries as reference, the growth rate of current financial revenue in China is higher or even much higher than the general international level.

It further inspires us that, in the world, the growth rate 8.1 percent of financial revenue can be considered as a good sign in normal state.

## "Practicing austerity" means "practice normality"

According to the previous discussion of the declining growth of financial revenue in current China, the basic conclusion can be reached that after the high-speed or even super-speed growth of financial revenue for almost 30 years, accompanying with the shift of economic growth, the growth of financial revenue must shift, too. It means that, under the macro-background that economy in China is entering a new stage of development, the financial revenue in China has already gone away from a special developmental period to a normal track. In this sense, it is inevitable that the growth of financial revenue declines. Therefore, the belief that the government should "practice austerity" means it should "practice normality".

If we realize that the growth of financial revenue in China has fallen back to a new platform and it is irreversible, it has to practice normality from the perspective of "normal thought" and make suitable arrangements about financial revenue and expenditure as well as make corresponding policies. At least the following aspects are included:

First, since the macroeconomic situation changes greatly, oversized government expenditure is bad for both economic structural adjustment and for sustainable and healthy economic development, so it is necessary to stabilize the existing proportion of government expenditure in GDP and try to prevent this proportion from rising. It means that the governments at all levels should economize to control general expenditure strictly that money should be spent where needed most. Moreover, even for the public investment expenditure which has to be spent, it should focus on the fields of infrastructure which are the base, promote long-term interests, benefit peoples' livelihoods and avoid redundant construction; meanwhile, it should also increase and guide private investment to enter these fields.

Second, because economic structural optimization is an important topic with important potential for economic development in China; because the fundamental way to solve the problems of excess capacity and economic structural adjustment is to transform government function thoroughly; and because it is necessary to adjust and optimize the structure of government expenditure further while stabilizing the existing proportion of government expenditure in GDP, the traditional thought must be given up that economic growth can be achieved by enlarging government expenditure and construction expenditure. The policy about government expenditure should also incline to peoples' livelihoods.

Third, because the pressure about financial revenue and expenditure in current China closely relates to current nonstandard government budget management, and "open, transparent, standard, and complete" have become important aims for government budget system reform, it is necessary to deepen financial tax system reform completely, standardizing government income and expenses and its mechanism completely. It means that the next step of financial and tax system reform must envisage and break the obstacles mainly coming from vested interests within the government and reformers must make up their minds to carry out government budget management with "full coverage" thoroughly. The current pressure of financial revenue and expenditure should be eased and defused by great dividends created and released by financial system reform.

Fourth, since the operation framework of macroeconomic policy in China has been adjusted significantly, and the focus of macroeconomic policy in current China is "stabilization", it is very necessary to keep continuousness and stabilization of the policies. On this basis, the government should stabilize the market and release certain signals to promote economic structural adjustment. It means that, facing the "double shifts" of both economic growth and financial revenue growth, it must keep calm to stick to proactive fiscal policy and prudent monetary policy. So long as the macroeconomy stays in reasonable range and is covered by active regulation, the pressure of financial revenue and expenditure and the change of financial situation mustn't be the reason to adjust macroeconomic policy greatly. With stable patterns of fiscal policy and monetary policy, it should let the market learn self-regulation, and leave enough space for the market to self-regulate, and further create market environment with fair competition, laying a solid foundation for a market which plays a decisive role in the allocation of resources.

(Originally published in *People's Daily*, October 24th, 2013)

# 12 Promotion of local government debt to the "new normal" by in-depth reform

## Local government debt risk: an unprecedentedly complicated situation

At present, the local government debt in China is still within the internationally recognized safety line when calculated according to national economic and financial strength. Though it is not enough to worry about in the overall scale, if we get rid of the overall view and deeply focus on various areas, we'll find that there are actually partial risks under the controllable overall risk, because some areas have been faced with difficulties in repayment with potential risks due to great differences in the regional economic development situation, management level and control degree of local government debt. If we get rid of the short-term view and focus on the long-term trend, we'll also find that there is actually long-term risk under the controllable short-term risk, because the severe situations in partial areas are likely to extend throughout the country, due to the continuous impact of various systemic factors deeply hidden behind the local government debt risk.

It is noteworthy that this kind of partial risk and long-term risk concerning the local government debt occurs when China's economy experiences turning changes and transforms into "new normal". It has three basic features. First, with the rapid growth over the past 30 years, the industrial structure and elements supporting the economic growth in China have changed, and China's economy has turned from a high-rate to a medium- and high-rate growth level. Second, the adjustment of economic structure by solving the problem of excess capacity has to be at the cost of mergers, involving reorganization and even withdrawal of enterprises from the market. Third, there has been continuous cumulative and spillover effect caused by the stimulus policies implemented since 2008, which reduces the space for selecting and controlling macroeconomic policies.

In the new trend known as "three phases" intended to simultaneously deal with the slowdown in economic growth, make difficult structural adjustments and absorb the effects of previous economic stimulus policies, on the one hand, the local government debt risk is interwoven with unprecedented new contradictions and problems; on the other hand, there is a series of unprecedented new issues and new challenges facing prevention and solution of the local government debt risk, thus showing an extremely complicated situation. As the growth rate of fiscal revenue decreases with the slowdown in economic growth, and the fiscal expenditure pressure increases with the difficult structural adjustment, there have been narrowing channels for the incremental adjustment under the increasingly severe situation of fiscal revenue and expenditure. In a relatively constrained macroeconomic situation, it has been increasingly hard to make breakthroughs in the vested interest pattern, because there are not only multiple constraints for choosing macro policies due to absorbing the effects of previous stimulus policies, but also a lot of challenges in front of the traditional mechanisms and approaches of macroeconomic regulation and control due to the further increasing pressure of economic downturn. With the considerable uncertainty in the institutional environment, it has been increasingly difficult to take countermeasures against risks, not only because the economy is experiencing turning changes and we haven't understood the law of economic system operating in such a situation yet, but also because in the process of comprehensive in-depth reform, there are also changes in various systems involving economy, politics, culture, society, ecological civilization, the Party building, etc.

## Special perspectives: identifying the root cause of local government debt risk

It is a common sense that local government debt is neither adverse nor peculiar to China. There have been success stories of indebted economic development in the history of China and many other countries. However, once we observe the current local government debt in China from a special perspective beyond the general perspective, we'll easily find that the current local government debt in China has been formed and evolved under a very special institutional background, which is exactly the root cause of the risk and various problems.

Special Perspective I: Intense debt demands are caused by the strong urge of investment promotion.

It can be learned through observation that local governments in China today have intense debt demands. Almost all local governments never give up any opportunity or possibility of debt financing, and are never satisfied.

Of course, intense debt demands are caused by strong investment demands, and strong investment demands are caused by the incorrect achievement view focusing on the pursuit of GDP. In this relational chain under a very special institutional background, the fierce competition in investment promotion among local governments has actually become a main driving force supporting the high-rate growth of China's economy over the past 30 years.

In order to attract investment, the government has to pay the price and surrender certain benefits. What are the means taken by local governments to attract investment?

Before the turning point in 1994, local government mainly attracted investment by abusing tax preferences. Thus, in that period, the competition in investment promotion among local governments was mainly reflected in the competition in amount of tax preference offered to investors.

As the financial and taxation reform was implemented in 1994, the gate of abusing tax preference was locked under the banner of unified tax law. Therefore, unauthorized fees began to replace the tax preference. Local governments attracted investment by new means of charging unauthorized fees from enterprises and residents to acquire additional funds, so as to offer various realistic and potential favorable terms for external investment.

Under the impact of waves of the "tax-for-fees" reform and the taxes and fees reform, the gate of collecting unauthorized fees had been closed by the end of the late 1990s. Local governments continually had to find other ways out to attract investment. Thus, land sales emerged and become popular with local governments who began to gain additional revenue through state-owned land transfer, so as to offer infrastructure and various public facilities for external investment.

There have been new changes in the situation since the beginning of 2008. On the one hand, with the implementation of "public land leasing" policy, state-owned land transfer has been standardized gradually. On the other hand, with the impact of the international financial crisis on China, we need to take inflationary economic measures to cope with the crisis and ensure growth. As the demand for investment promotion of local government is integrated with the anti-crisis policy, the debt from various local financing platforms has begun to spring up. Taking the advantage of the anti-crisis policy, local governments could not only get rid of the current budget system in which debt financing is not allowed for local governments, but also openly attract external investment and create favorable conditions for investment promotion through government investment, so as to drive the growth of GDP. As a result, there has been a growth spurt in the scale of local government debt.

Through such a general review, it is observed that the local debt today is actually caused by the earlier abuse of tax preference as well as the previous collection of unauthorized fees and non-normative state-owned land transfer. The logical path of local government debt of seeking development → making achievements → launching projects → increasing investment → taking a free ride in debt financing, reminds us that, though the problem is reflected in local government debt, its root cause lies in the infinite and blind pursuit of investment promotion led by the unshakable status of GDP. Demands of local governments for debt financing will be infinite unless this root cause is removed. As long as the special institutional factor exists, the local government debt will certainly cause some risks sooner or later, and even cause high risks which are enough to threaten the national long-term stability.

Special Perspective II: A debtor's unsound personality is caused by the unsound fiscal management system.

It is originally a basic principle of the human society that debts should be paid. However, the principle is not applicable to the debt financing behavior of Chinese local governments. All the survey results from various fields show that in China today, not a few local governments have no intention to repay the debt during debt financing, and no corresponding liquidity during repayment. In other words, the current local governments are debtors with unsound personality.

What's the problem? At root, the formation of a debtor's unsound personality is directly related to the unsound fiscal management system pattern. As far as the current fiscal management system in China is concerned, though it holds the banner of "tax-sharing system" nominally, it actually has deviated from the course of "tax-sharing system".

In the proper sense, the "tax-sharing fiscal management system" at least has three layers of meaning: "power-sharing, tax-sharing and management-sharing": The "power-sharing" refers to dividing the responsibilities of fiscal expenditure at all levels based on the division of responsibility (administrative power) scope among governments at all levels on the premise that the functional boundary among governments has been defined. The "tax-sharing" refers to dividing the taxes between the central government and local governments into several categories, including central tax, local tax and tax shared by the central and local governments, following the principle of unity between financial power and administrative power on the basis that administrative power and expenditure scope have been divided, so as to delimit the source of revenue to the central government and local governments. The "management-sharing" refers to implementing the level-to-level fiscal management on the bases of power-sharing and tax-sharing. The government and budget subject at the first level, as well as the budget at all levels, are relatively independent, pursuing the balance respectively.

Contrasting that meaning to the operation pattern of the current fiscal management system, we can easily learn that there have always been large gaps between the current situation and the real sense of "power-sharing", "tax-sharing" and "management-sharing" during the past 20 years. In fact, the gaps are still extending even though a series of so-called adaptability adjustments have been implemented. The situation is typically reflected in that 70 percent of central financial expenditure should be allocated to local government as tax returns and transfer payment, while about 50 percent of local fiscal revenue depends on the central financial allocation. Furthermore, most of about 50 percent of the appropriations belongs to the directly-allocated special transfer payment, and even the general transfer payment also to a great extent has the uncertainty of "access to funds by means of the relationship with departments of various ministries and commissions".

Local governments achieve the balance between revenue and expenditure by highly relying on the central finance in an institutional environment with considerable uncertainty, which may lead the local fiscal revenue and expenditure system to an incomplete status, and cause long-term difficulty with local finance. It's only natural that local governments struggle to fully take the responsibilities of their own revenue and expenditure activities as sound behavior subjects when they fail to fully control their revenue and expenditure operations. In the long term, not only does the basis for implementing level-to-level fiscal management tend to be weak, but also the sound personality of a fiscal subject at the first level inevitably degrades. As a result, it will still be controllable if debt financing is not allowed for local governments with intense debt demands but without self-discipline. However, once the others-discipline constraint to debt financing is loosened slightly, local governments are very likely to be trapped into a whirlpool of blind debt financing like those children out of control.

According to the logic chain concerning local governments featured by institutional environment deviating from "tax-sharing system" → unsound fiscal revenue and expenditure system → unsound behavior subjects → debtor's unsound personality → blind debt financing, we can recognize that though the problem is reflected in the local government debt, its root cause lies in the fiscal management system pattern deviating from the course of "tax-sharing system". As long as the local fiscal revenue and expenditure system is unsound, local governments are hardly able to become sound behavior subjects, and thus hardly able to become debtors with sound personality. The local government debt cannot get rid of the "risk" unless the institutional environment is changed thoroughly. The risk will come sooner or later, even though there is no risk today.

## Remedy: treating both symptoms and causes of the local debt by in-depth reform

It is imperative to notice the actual situation that the local government debt is extremely complex during the transition to the "new normal" of economy, recognize that various systemic chronic diseases deeply hidden behind the local government debt is exactly the root cause of various real and potential risks, and change the way of thinking to prevent and relieve the local government debt risk and solve the problem of local government debt. The only choice for us is to first deepen the reform to remedy the situation, and take major reform measures considering planning both local and overall, and short-term and long-term.

Therefore, we can make a strategic choice to designate pilot local governments that issue and repay bonds by themselves as a starting point and a breakthrough, and then promote the reform to the level involving performance evaluation and the fiscal revenue and expenditure system of local governments, so as to steadily and smoothly achieve the transition of local government debt operation to the "new normal" by comprehensively deepening the reform.

First, we should lay an emphasis on reform of the fundamental system, and actively promote the work on pilot local governments that issue and repay bonds by themselves. In any case, as fiscal and behavior subjects of the governments at the first level, local governments should have the right of debt financing. From all perspectives, the debt financing of local governments is a necessary measure for accelerating economic development. Thus, it's better to relieve the local government debt, rather than put it to an end. We only need to strengthen the management of the local government debt when relieving the issue. In fact, when we strive for finding a solution for the issue, it's possible to find a proper management way of the local government debt applicable to the situation of China only through those reform activities such as the pilot local governments that issue and repay bonds by themselves, so as to reveal various problems related to the local government debt including partial and long-term risks.

What seems to be the trouble is that the measure of designating pilot local governments that issue and repay bonds by themselves only belongs to technical adjustment intended for relieving the current contradictions, rather than a fundamental reform. In other words, the measure can only affect the external manifestation of the local government debt problem at most, rather than its internal core contents. Therefore, the measure of designating pilot local governments that issue and repay bonds by themselves should ultimately aim to approach to the systemic chronic diseases of the local government debt problem, starting from the surface to the center.

Second, we should set up a modern performance evaluation system for local governments in line with state governance by eradicating the old and fostering the new in the meantime.

As governments at the first level, there are no grounds to blame local governments for pursuing their performance. However, the pursuit of performance shouldn't be limited to GDP anyhow, and shouldn't even be implemented for the infinite and blind pursuit of investment promotion. Considering that there has been a set of subtle thinking and operation systems focusing on GDP assessment in China, but no system and mechanism has been created based on the needed extensive consensus to replace the original evaluation system, it is necessary to adhere to eradicating the old and fostering the new in the meantime of weakening and abolishing the GDP assessment. There has also been no change in the performance evaluation of local governments and their officials integrated with the reforms of the economic, political, cultural, social, ecological civilization and Party-building systems from an overall perspective of promoting the modernization of state governance, so as to set up an institutional system required by and applicable to the comprehensive performance evaluation of local governments at root.

On this basis, local governments can get out of the strange circle where they mainly compete for the investment promotion focusing on GDP as an unshakable role, so as to step onto the right track for achieving performance.

Third, we should put the emphasis on improving the local fiscal systems so as to reconstruct the tax-sharing fiscal system pattern.

Different from the finance of the budget unit, the basic connotation of the first-level government finance is that it also has two kinds of rights of property: relatively independent revenue and expenditure management rights, and relatively independent revenue and expenditure balance rights. These two kinds of property rights undoubtedly should be established as the basis of a sound financial revenue and expenditure system. In other words, the local finance without the support of sound financial revenue and expenditure system must be the one that can't independently exercise the revenue and expenditure management right as well as the revenue and expenditure balance right, and it's certainly not the local finance under the financial system pattern of tax-sharing in its original meaning. Needless to say, the adherence of the reform direction of "tax-sharing" perfects the local financial revenue and expenditure system through the reconstruction of the financial system pattern of tax-sharing, which is the premise that allows the local governments to have a sound debtor personality.

In the face of the daunting task of perfecting the local financial revenue and expenditure systems and restructuring the financial system pattern of tax-sharing, it's obviously very necessary to clarify and establish the following basic understandings:

First, the tax-sharing system is the system for money distribution. As the same as the actual content of rural reform, namely to change the "food distribution" to "field distribution" in 1994, the means of reform in implementing the financial system of "tax-sharing system" was the "system for money distribution", and no matter whether it's sharing in the total revenue, sharing in income classification or mismatching cost, it's essentially the "system of money distribution". Thus, on the basis of the division of the central tax, local tax and shared central and local tax, it's one of the basic features of the tax-sharing system to let the central and local governments maintain or own a sound budget system and live their lives in a relatively stable system.

Second, the level-to-level management of finance is not "pass-by finance". Just like the truth that the budget unit is different from the first-level government finance, the level-to-level management of finance in such a big country can't be based on the assignment of corresponding funds according to the matters engaged. Otherwise, the level-to-level management of finance is likely to degenerate into the financial management of budget units, or the level-to-level management of finance is likely to be degenerated into single-level financial management. Therefore, the central and local levels of perfect financial revenue and expenditure systems are established respectively according to the principle of level-to-level management of finance. Living their own lives under the system of level-to-level management is one of the basic premise to implement the level-to-level financial management.

Third, the taxation right is not equal to the property right. In China of a single system, it is necessary for us to emphasize that the tax legislative power is highly concentrated with the central government. However, the high concentration of the legislative power of taxation does not mean that the financial management right can't be delegated to local government. Instead, on the premise of insisting that the tax legislative power is highly concentrated, it's not only one of the necessary conditions to implement the level-to-level financial management, but also to implement a financial tax-sharing system by granting local government financial management power with relatively independent organizational revenue and expenditure and balanced revenue and expenditure.

(Originally published in *Guangming Daily*,
September 10, 2014)

# 13  Profound knowledge in the "new normal" of finance

The analysis and judgment of the current economic situation can't be separated from the financial situation. As one of the most comprehensive economic indicators, the financial situation is still an important observation point.

In accordance with the calculation of general public budget revenue, the national fiscal revenue in 2014 was 14.034974 trillion Yuan, an increase of 8.6 percent over 2013. Compared with the 7.4 percent GDP growth of same period, it seems a plausible number. However, after the deep analysis of the actual contents, it would be extremely alerting.

The revenue growth of 8.6 percent was realized based on taking a series of special measures of adding the income of some financial institutions. If we ignore the decline of growth momentum of fiscal revenue but do not take the initiatives, it won't reach such a level of growth and is extremely unlikely to achieve the budget target of 8 percent national fiscal revenue growth in 2014. This is the first point.

Looking back to the "Eleventh Five-Year Plan" period, the average annual revenue growth was 21.3 percent, nearly 10 percent higher than the GDP growth rate over the same period. Even after entering the "Twelfth Five-Year Plan", in 2011, the national financial revenue growth rate reached 25 percent, and fell from 25 percent down to 8.6 percent in 2014, in only three years – the decline had big momentum, and it's definitely a rare example in the history of the world's financial development. This is the second point.

The declining rate further sped up this year. In January, the national fiscal revenue growth was only 3.4 percent, lower than the GDP growth rate over the same period, and you may notice that the normal state of the operation of financial income in the past years is "high first, low later". This year, we will strive to complete the "replacement of the business tax with value-added tax" by sacrificing about RMB 400 billion of taxes, and further implement tax cuts to small and micro enterprises. Under these conditions, you can imagine how difficult it is to complete the budget target of 7.3 percent growth in the national fiscal revenue this year. This is the third point.

In China, more than 20 percent or even 30 percent revenue growth has been maintained for many years, and people have become accustomed to apportioning the "surplus" income and improvement of benefits every year. For a long time, under the control of a series of institutional factors, China has not set up a mechanism that fiscal expenditure is automatically reduced with the decrease of fiscal income as exists in Europe, the United States and other countries. In fact, in sharp contrast to the decline in the growth rate of fiscal revenue, whether in the last year or this year, the growth rate of fiscal expenditure has no substantial cut. The huge pressure caused by the sharp contrast of financial revenue and expenditure should not be underestimated. This is the fourth point.

Looking at the overall situation and disregarding local gains and losses, if necessary, we would rather exchange the economic and social stability and development with imbalance of financial revenue and expenditure, which has been the basic principle of China in selecting the fiscal policies since the reform and opening-up policy. Based on the needs of maintaining growth, in the past year, the government made efforts by a series of expansionary actions of reduction in income and increase in expenditure. In this year, facing the grim situation of continuous economic downward pressure and increased threat of deflation, the boosting efficiency of proactive fiscal policy is imperative. Undoubtedly, it will further increase the pressure of reduction in income and increase in expenditure, making the financial operation in a tight state this year. This is the fifth point.

Above all, these are serious ramifications of the current financial situation. In this regard, we can't let down, but need to make new judgments with new ideas and new perspectives. We should view it from the perspective of financial revenue and expenditure and place it in the background of the new normal of economic development. The following understanding and conclusions may be appropriate:

First, economy determines finance, which is a basic law that has long been known to people. After more than 30 years of reform and opening-up policy, China's economy has entered the new normal of development. As the demographic dividend decreased and the labor costs increased, the adjustment to vigorously develop service industries inevitably leads to the growth of social labor productivity and the slowdown of overall economic growth rate. In other words, as China enters the stage from rapid growth to a medium and high-speed growth and single-digit growth, the growth rate of fiscal revenue will naturally be reduced.

Second, the high-speed and even ultra-high speed growth phenomenon of China's fiscal revenue continued for many years after 1994. Prior to this, we also experienced a sustained decline in revenue growth over the years. The V-shaped curve of fiscal revenue over 30 years at least tells us two basic facts. First, the continued rapid growth of fiscal revenue after 1994 to a large extent was the correction of continuously declining fiscal revenue growth, which had a considerable compensation in nature. Since it is a compensation, this compensation will not be endless. After the compensation reaches a node, it is bound to return to the normal track. Second, the continued rapid growth of fiscal revenue after 1994 can be attributed to a large extent to the product of fiscal reform in 1994, which included a considerable nature of reform dividend. Since it is the reform dividend, the release of this dividend effect will not be amplified continuously. After the dividend effect is released for some time, it must step into a state of decline. That is to say, the sustained and rapid growth of financial revenue – especially the growth of financial revenue higher than, and even far higher than, the economic growth – is a special phenomenon of the development stage. Only the adaptation of fiscal revenue growth to economic growth is the new normal in life.

Third, the main body of China's financial revenue is tax revenue. Under China's current tax system, more than 70 percent of the tax revenue is from value-added tax, business tax, consumption tax and other indirect taxes. The pattern of tax revenue "leaning to indirect tax" means that most tax revenues in China should be included in the price as elements of the price. It is not only tied together with the goods and service prices, but also increases and decreases with the ups and downs of the price, and is volatile with slight changes in the price. When the economy increases rapidly, the growth rate of tax revenue may be higher than the economic growth. When the slowdown in economic growth is lower than the growth rate in the past, the growth rate of tax revenue may be lower than the economic growth rate. Therefore, as long as China's current tax system and the real tax revenue pattern decided by it don't change, it's a surprise that the slowdown of China's economic growth will bring a larger decline of tax revenue and fiscal revenue.

Fourth, the calculation of general account of macroeconomic and social development and the realization of overall benefits with the boosting efficiency of finance are, of course, the price that the economy must pay. However, this does not mean that we have no idea to cope with the possible pressure and difficulties we may face to achieve macroeconomic goals. Instead, we should conduct comprehensive and detailed analysis of various factors affecting the fiscal revenue and expenditures as far as possible, adopt early plans and take proactive actions to face the risks based on this, which can ensure relevant decisions and measures more stable and reliable. That's to say, considering that the current proactive fiscal policy is initiated against the background that economic development enters a new normal, transitional changes occur in fiscal situations and it aims at expansion actions to stimulate the economy, the current round of proactive fiscal policy should find a new way out, different from the past.

It can be considered that the grim situation of fiscal revenue and expenditure caused by the decline of current financial revenue growth is not only the fact that we have to accept, but also the product of the law of economic development. The current austere life or hardship is actually a normal financial day, or with respect to the old normal of loose life in the past, the austere life and bitter life are the new normal of the economy in China.

In the face of all these changes, we must adjust our philosophy, psychology, strategy and policy comprehensively, learn to live in the new normal, coexist with the new normal, and implement the focus of current financial routines and fiscal policy operations on the track of entering the new normal of finance with a series of actions different from the past and taking the initiative to adapt to and lead the new normal.

(Originally published in *Economic Daily*, March 13, 2015)

# Index

Page numbers in italic indicate a figure on the corresponding page.

For Product Safety Concerns and Information please contact our EU
representative GPSR@taylorandfrancis.com
Taylor & Francis Verlag GmbH, Kaufingerstraße 24, 80331 München, Germany